Tom Doorley
Uncorked!

ON STREAM

Published 1995 by On Stream Publications Ltd. Cloghroe, Blarney, Co. Cork. Ireland.   Tel 021 385798 Fax 021 385798

ISBN:1 897685 89 0

Cover photograph: Gillian Treacy at First Degree Photography taken at Karwigs Wine Warehouse, Carrigaline, Co.Cork.

Printed in Dublin by Colour Books.

Wines listed are available countrywide unless otherwise specified

Prices are correct at time of publication. The publisher does not accept liability for any changes occurring thereafter.

It's amazing how we in Ireland persist in drinking wine - despite constant discouragement from successive governments. I like to think that it tells us something about our national character. But the fact remains that we suffer the highest taxation on wine in the EU. It would be nice to think that someday soon we will pay the same as our neighbours in the United Kingdom - which has the second highest wine tax in Europe. At least it would be a move in the right direction.

Slowly but surely we are becoming a nation of wine drinkers and Irish consumers want to know more about what lies behind the label and that's the main reason I decided to write this book. It's designed to be a handy guide to the vast majority of wine you will find on the supermarket and off-licence shelves. Needless to say, it's a highly personal view and I certainly don't expect everyone to agree with the opinions expressed here. I know, for example, many people of irreproachable character to actually like Muscadet. Weird but true!

Two years ago when I produced the first annual Sunday Tribune Wine Guide I said that it was written purely for you, the consumer. The same is true of this book. Not everybody in the wine trade will be entirely happy with Tom Doorley Uncorked and that, frankly, is as it should be. Having said that, I want to pay tribute to the wine trade for all their help and encouragement to me over the ten years I've been writing about wine. I couldn't have done it without them.

I want to thank two people in particular for helping me make this book a reality: Peter Murtagh of The Sunday Tribune, and Roz Crowley of On Stream who took on the arduous task of translating an idea of mine into what you're now holding in your hands.

Finally, a word about my approach to wine. Wine, let's not forget, is an agricultural product whether it's made by small farmers or giant cooperatives. It's made, for the most part, to accompany food and it's certainly not for wineupmanship. Above all wine is, quite simply for fun. And I hope you have fun with this little book. Tom Doorley

RECOMMENDED WINE SHOPS

Dublin
Deveney's(DV) 01 295 1745: Good value off-licences with a reasonable range.
Ecock's(E) 01 283 1664: Italian specialists.
Findlater's(F) 01 475 1699: Superb range of serious wines, available by mixed case.
McCabe's(McC) 01 288 2037/833 5277: Possibly the capital's best off-licence, serious about wine.
Mitchell's (MI)01 676 0766: Delightful shop, serious wine merchants, excellent German and Portuguese ranges.)
Molloy's(MO)01 451 4857: A chain to watch with a serious commitment to interesting wines.
O'Brien's(O'B) 01 269 3033: Down-to-earth, good values with some very serious Germans and clarets.
Searson's(SN)01 280 0405: Treasure trove of fine wines, one of the best merchants in the country with small retail shop in Monkstown.
Redmond's(R)01 497 1739: Traditional off-licence with very extensive range.
Terroirs 01 667 1311: Upmarket wine and food shop with many gems and some very reasonably priced wines.
Verlings(V)01 833 1653: Excellent range of wines and knowledgeable staff.
Cork
Karwig Wines(K) 021 372864): Vast eclectic range with particular strengths in Italy and Germany.
Pomeroy's(P) 021 274753: A real enthusiast's wine shop with some rarities.
Waterford
The Wine Vault(WV) 051 53444: A marvellous collection, including some very serious New World contenders.
Limerick
Fine Wines(FW) 061 417784: A very sound, well-stocked shop with a fine claret selection.
Galway
McCambridge's(McC) 091 562259: Well-established wine section in fine old food shop.
Merchant's Wine Club(MW) 091 561833: Staggering range of wines selected with insatiable enthusiasm. Very strong on Burgundy and New World.
Northern Ireland
Direct Wine Shipments, Belfast (DWS) 0801232 24390: A great selection of wines including good claret, Chapoutier and Hugel and vintage ports.
James Nicholson, Crossgar(JN) 0801396 830091: One of the country's finest ranges with great Californian and German curiosities.
Supermarkets:
Dunne's Stores(DS), Superquinn(SQ), SuperValu(SV), Quinnsworth(QW)

Mail Order: Wines Direct(WD): Small, quality conscious business with particular strengths in Bordeaux and the Pays d'Oc.

AUSTRALIA

They're big, bouncy and full of fruit and that's the way we like our wine in Ireland. Secondly, they're easy to pronounce (try comparing Jacob's Creek with Pacherenc du Vic Bilh and you will see what I mean). Finally - and this is what appeals to our fundamentally rebellious nature - they're not French!

Collective folk memories of snooty little men with waxed moustaches getting all precious and Gallic and superior over a pathetic bottle of Beaujolais make the g'day style of everyday Australian wine folk rather appealing. I find the main difference between Australian and European wine makers is very simple. You ask them how they make their wine - and one explains that it's all down to his ancestors, the unique *terroir* and God. The other just tells you. No prizes for guessing which is which.

Australia is hotter than Bordeaux and grapes can reach staggering degrees of ripeness. While the Europeans worry about getting as much sun as possible, Australians try to devise ways of combating it. Choosing relatively cool sites and training vine leaves over the grapes - canopy management - are two techniques that they use.

If you look at a map of the wine regions of Australia you may be surprised to see how the vine is concentrated in just a few areas. Essentially you have South-Eastern Australia, about a thousand miles across, which stretches from Adelaide in the West to the Hunter Valley north of Sydney.

The Barossa Valley is celebrated for its Shiraz and Riesling, Coonawarra for its Cabernet which thrives on its red, iron-rich soil, Padthaway for its Chardonnay and the Hunter for long-lived Semillon. The cool Eden Valley, north of Adelaide, is producing exceptional Pinot Noir. In Western Australia, wine activity is concentrated around Perth which has more millionaires than any other city in Australia. This, combined with a cool climate and a small average size for the wineries, probably explains why wines from Western Australia tend to be on the dear side.

Traditionally Australian wine was thick, jammy, oxidised and flabby - all because of the heat. Orlando started a revolution when they imported special equipment from Germany in the 1950s. Suddenly, Australia had its first temperature-controlled, stainless steel winery and the result was...well, it was a semi-sparkling wine called Barossa Pearl, a kind of downunder Mateus Rosé of the early 1960s but it was a start. Before you could say Koonunga Hill, the message had spread.

Cool and carefully controlled fermentation means that the Australians could capture the fruity characteristics of their very, very ripe fruit. And everybody loved it. The export market was a bit slow to catch on but then the UK chain Oddbins took the bull by the horns and bought up whopping quantities of Australian wine in 1986/87. They piled it high and sold it cheap. Britain was captivated.

Ireland followed suit a little later, Rosemount being first off the blocks. It was left to O'Brien's, the Dublin off-licence chain, however, to show that Australian wine could be both cheerful and cheap. They built a huge following for Jacob's Creek until the brand was bought by Groupe Pernod Ricard, owners of Irish Distillers, and it moved agents.

Jacob's Creek had been selling at £4.99. Irish Distillers surprised the trade by holding to that price point and within months sales had gone into orbit. The launch of a pure Chardonnay at the same price set a new standard for cheaper wines and soon Jacob's Creek had become what Distillers coyly describe as 'the biggest take-home brand in Ireland'.

Even those who are inclined to frown a little on Jacob's Creek (nothing breeds contempt like success) will admit that at least people were now drinking real wine rather than the kind of gunk that had previously dominated the branded wine sector. And Irish wine consumers never looked back.

True, the cheaper Australians are not quite what they were - because of soaring demand and poor harvests - but we have learned that we like the up-front, well-upholstered nature of these down-to-earth wines. What we are slower to appreciate is that there are Australian wines which offer amazing complexity and excitement. Sadly, we expect them to cost a pittance. Life, I'm afraid, isn't like that. Even in Australia.

1996 will be the toughest year yet for Australian wine. There are serious shortages of grapes for all kinds of wine but the big brands will be worst hit. Currency fluctuations may also force price increases and the big, flavourful new wave wines from southern France - many of them made by Australians - are poised to mop up a lot of the market. But however good they are, they have one disadvantage. None of them is called anything even remotely like Billabong Creek or Tuckerbag Ridge. It's an idea, though, isn't it? 'Le Gout de Sweaty Saddle, Cabernet Sauvignon, Vin de Pays d'Oc,' has a certain ring to it.

BUZZ WORDS are big in the New World. Here are a few that can be thrown casually into the conversation when you meet your neighbourhood wine bore.

Canopy management: Vine leaves grown over the grapes to keep them cool in the baking Australian sun.
Riesling: The smart Australian money is on this shamefully neglected grape variety.
Tarrango: Australia's very own grape variety (see below).
Clonal selection: They clone vines and yeast varieties downunder which explains a lot of the consistency (or, in extreme cases, awful sameness).
Tropical fruits: That's what certain cloned yeasts smell of.
Tasmania: A cool-climate region on the brink of major success with serious whites and Pinot Noir.

WINERY PROFILES

Angove's make decent commercial wines around Renmark in South Australia and their Shiraz Classic Reserve 1992 (O'B £6.45) is a simple, dark, plummy mouthful at the price - exclusive to O'Brien's.

d'Arenberg is a fairly recent winery, based in McLaren Vale, South Australia. Despite their rather dull and unattractive labels, I think the wines all impressive. I first encountered the spicy, concentrated Old Vine McLaren Vale Shiraz 1990 (£9.90) and the stylish Barrel-Fermented Chardonnay 1993 (£9.90) in Adelaide where they more than held their own in the biggest Australian tasting I've ever attended.

Bailey's of Glenrowan make one of the most luscious, concentrated, long and complex fortified dessert wines, Bailey's Liqueur Muscat (McC £16.99). Expect a taste of figs, raisins, dates, nuts, citrus fruit, tawny port and liquorice all rolled into one mind-blowing glassful. However, it seems that Bailey's Irish Cream (which, if you remember, is said to have been invented in Soho in 1976) is objecting to the name. The Australian Bailey's, incidentally, have been selling wine since 1870 - more than a century before the wonders of cream liqueur was unleashed upon an unsuspecting world. Now owned by Rothbury Estates but still the supreme Muscat people.

Berri Estates make vast quantities of good wine, mainly in the irrigated Murray River region. Star players include their scrumptiously fresh and fruity Unwooded Chardonnay (O'B £6.99). In an age when everybody seems to think that oak is essential it's good to see a label proclaiming that the nearest thing to wood this wine has touched is a stainless steel tank. The basic Dry Plains (O'B £4.99) range are pleasant enough glugging wine at the price.

Wolf Blass is one of Australia's best self-publicists and even he would never claim that modesty is his middle name. This German immigrant who bears an uncanny resemblance to Ronnie Corbett makes textbook

Australian wines all of which are good, from the relatively cheap red label range (£7.99) where the star is the clean, fresh yet fleshy Semillon, through to the voluptuous Cabernet Sauvignon President's Selection 1990 (£12.00) with its layers of ripe fruit and toasty, vanilla-like oak. When I want to drink what I consider to be the essence of Australian red wine - whopping fruit, lots of vanilla-and-spice, considerable softness and lushness counterbalanced by firm, ripe tannins - this is a wine I often seek out. Sure, it lacks subtlety but it's great fun. The rare and expensive Black Label Cabernet Sauvignon/Shiraz1990 (QW £19.99) is huge, eccentric, and fabulously concentrated - and, yes, probably worth the money. Wolf Blass wines may not be as good as the man thinks - but for most mortals they will do nicely.

Barramundi wines (£6.14) come from the best producer in Riverina - but there is no real competition. Nice people, pretty label, very ordinary wine.

De Bortoli's best wine is the Botrytis Affected Semillon known also as Noble One (SQ £10.99 per half bottle) which is so rich, sweet, concentrated and impressive that Lindeman's have been known to buy it to sell under their own label. Ignore De Bortoli's Riverina wines (and anybody else's too - Riverina is Australia's bulk wine capital and alleged Mafia stronghold) and look for evidence that the stuff comes from their Victoria estates, for example the medium-price Windy Peak wines. This is very different, very high quality, especially their Shiraz.

Brown Brothers just keep surprising me. They have always made brilliant sweet and dry Muscats, but latterly their Chardonnays, Cabernets and Shirazes have come on by leaps and bounds. Their Late Picked Muscat 1993 (£7.99) is one of the most attractive and affordable dessert wines commonly available: light, grapey, aromatic, low in alcohol and really honeyed with the sweetness well-balanced by crisp acidity. Brown Brothers Orange Flora and Muscat (£6.99 per half bottle) is utterly delicious: low in alcohol, grapey, floral, sweet yet nicely sharp on the tongue. Orange Flora, incidentally, refers to a modest grape variety not to the citrus character you sometimes get with certain Muscat wines. Their Dry

Muscat 1993 (£7.79) makes a lovely aperitif or accompaniment to spicy food, while their King Valley Chardonnay 1993 (£9.99) is ripe, buttery, oaky yet underpinned by a refreshing, crisp acidity which lends just enough austerity to the wine. A few years ago Brown Brothers Tarrango 1994 (SQ £6.49) would have seemed a touch expensive by comparison to the juicy young Beaujolais it so closely resembles but the way prices are going it now looks like a snip - and you get a nice whack of tannin on the very finish which makes it a better food wine. Milawa in Victoria where Brown Brothers are based can be like an oven in the summer. You can taste the baked fruit in their stunning but hard-to-find Liqueur Muscat.

Cape Mentelle, named after the nearest coastal feature, produces serious and expensive wine in one of the cooler parts of Western Australia and is part-owned by Cloudy Bay of New Zealand - hence the similar labelling. (Incidentally, had Cloudy Bay been named with the same attention to geographical detail, it would have been called Farewell Spit). The Cabernet/Merlot 1991 (SQ £15.09) and the Chardonnay are classic, elegant, big wines with more than a touch of French influence. There's no doubt that cool growing conditions allied to traditional vinification make complex wines - even down here - although they don't merit more than three or four years ageing. The Semillon/ chardonnay which appears on quite a few fashionable restaurant lists is pleasant enough but perhaps a little over-priced.

Hardy's produce a huge range of excellent wines from all over Australia and I've never been really let down by any of them. However the Eileen Hardy Chardonnay 1990 (McC/R £13.99) and Eileen Hardy Shiraz 1989 (McC/R £13.99) are outstanding. The Chardonnay is from the classic white wine region of Padthaway, a kind of white wine Coonawarra, and has masses of really concentrated, rather aristocratic fruit coupled with toasty, elegant French oak. When I tasted the 1970 vintage of the Shiraz at their McLaren Vale winery I couldn't believe the youthful shape it was in - though I reckon the wines are now made with less structure and more emphasis on easy-drinking. By contrast, the fabulously intense and very accurately-titled E & E Black Pepper Shiraz (c.£17) is one of

Australia's great red wines, a kind of missing link between the Northern Rhone and the Barossa Valley. This peppery, almost black wine is made in tiny quantities and, yes, there's a pepper tree in the middle of the vineyard. Barossa Shiraz is famous and this is probably the best you can buy. It's on strict allocation so grab it if you happen to see it. This is one Australian red which will take as much as a decade in the cellar - perhaps more. Hardy's Nottage Hill (£5.99) wines are very honest and reasonably priced - and nicely oaked. The Stamp Series and the Bird Series are both leaders in their price categories.

Hill-Smith/Yalumba are remarkable in being a family firm which manages to produce a vast range of wines at different price and quality levels, none of them less than perfectly acceptable. The Old Triangle (£5.59) range of varietals are good, basic Oz wines with upfront fruit and uncomplicated flavours. I favour the Riesling with its green apple sharpness and faint touch of residual sugar which makes it a good companion for certain spicy Szechuan dishes. Hill-Smith Cabernet Sauvignon/Shiraz 1989 (F £8.99) is quite complex and certainly has some ageing potential.

The Heggies Estate wines (F £10.99) are outstanding, particularly the Eden Valley Botrytis Riesling (F £9.00 per half bottle) with its almost orange colour, intensely sweet yet crisp palate and that lovely, faintly petrol-scented nose. This superb dessert wine is being seen more often in good restaurants.

The Oxford Landing range is yet another string to the Yalumba bow and has opened up a new price point for Australian wine. The Cabernet/Shiraz (£6.69) is exactly what most people want: soft, easy and oaky. The Chardonnay (£6.69) is remarkably sophisticated for the price and the green, grassy Sauvignon Blanc (£6.69) is one of the few Australian examples of this varietal which captures a green, grassy, herbaceous character like we now expect from New Zealand. Yalumba Show Reserve Muscat (McC £8.99 per half bottle) is absolutely gorgeous - not quite so multi-layered as Bailey's but superb all the same. Cockatoo

Ridge Shiraz/Cabernet and Chardonnay (McC/R £6.49) is made with the help of legendary wine maker Geoff Merrill (whose moustache appears to have been grown under glass) and combines lovely fruit and oak flavours with a really modern, clean style. Very stylish and great value. Angas Brut (£7.99) was the first Australian fizz to hit these shores and splendid, unserious stuff it is too. It goes for exuberance rather than any degree of complexity and the pink version is still ahead of the white - although the gap in quality is closing. Cuvee One Prestige Pinot-Chardonnay (£12.99) is far and away Australia's finest sparkler, with amazingly biscuity Champagne-like style.

Jamieson's Run make very correct, commercial wines as part of the Mildara-Blass conglomerate but nothing outstanding.

Lindemans, part of the Penfolds empire, is one of Australia's famous names. I find the cheaper wines, sold under the Henry Lindemans label, rather ordinary and disappointing but the Chardonnay Bin 65 1994 (£6.99) is, to my mind, one of the best in its class. The Shiraz Bin 50 1993 (£6.99) and Cabernet Sauvignon Bin 45 1993 (£6.99) are both good, big, fruity wines with an elegant touch of oak on the finish. However, the Padthaway Chardonnay Reserve 1991 (SQ/R/QW £12.99) is a really great wine, one of Australia's most impressive whites with a wonderful integration of fruit, acid and oak. This is not a whopper. It's an elegant wine with terrific depth and the taste just goes on and on. The Coonawarra Cabernet Sauvignon Reserve 1989 (QW/R £12.99) is equally impressive with its rich mint and eucalyptus whiff combining with intense cassis. Single vineyards in Coonawarra yield impressive reds in the shape of St George's and Limestone Ridge, both capable of developing serious complexity with five to eight years bottle age. Expect to pay around £15 for them if you find them in an off-licence, and almost twice that in a restaurant. Pyrus (around £20) is a Cabernet/Merlot blend in a deliberately Bordeaux-style, surprisingly closed when young, but opening up beautifully after ten years or so.

Welcome newcomers are McWilliams Mount Pleasant Philip Hunter River Shiraz 1989 (QW £7.99) and the Elizabeth Hunter Valley Semillon 1990

(QW £7.99). The latter will improve in bottle for 20 or 30 years.

Mildara wines are not seen much in Ireland but it's worth keeping an eye open for their Balgownie wines which make up in intensity what they lack, perhaps, in finesse.

Mitchelton have a very beautiful estate in Victoria where they make an unusual melon-scented and delicately-oaked Marsanne 1993 (£7.99) using a classic Rhone varietal which is rarely seen in Australia. But their other wines don't send me into paroxysms of excitement. Their much-vaunted Preece Cabernet Sauvignon (DS £7.99) tastes just downright clumsy. Terribly pretty packaging, though. I have a feeling that Mitchelton is on the brink of doing great things, so it's certainly a producer to watch.

The Mountadam winery is in the appropriately heavenly Eden Valley above Adelaide where Adam Wynn makes amazingly stylish and complex Burgundian-style pinot and Chardonnay. He uses vast numbers of clones to ensure that the wines are multi-dimensional and his obses-sional winemaking results in some of Australia's very finest and most sur-prising wines. At around £16 a bottle they're not cheap but you would need to spend at least twice or three times that much to get the same buzz from Burgundy. They are exclusive to David Dennison's Wine Vault in Waterford.

Orlando make Jacob's Creek, the starting point for the Australian revolu-tion and, as such, it tends to be frowned on by certain fashion-conscious wine buffs. However, the wines offer remarkable consistency and Robin Day, the wine maker, is one of Australia's top gurus who is now oversee-ing wineries in places as diverse as Argentina and South Africa. The red is Shiraz/Cabernet (£4.99) with cool climate Cabernet introducing a dis-tinctive note in the background. The partly oak-fermented Chardonnay (£5.49) packs a tremendous amount of flavour for the price point but dur-ing 1996 it seems that they will have difficulty meeting demand. The Semillon/ chardonnay (£4.99) is more restrained, with somewhat crisper acidity, a less exotic aroma and a style I rather like. Together they make up in dependability and drinkability what some may claim they lack in sheer finesse and excitement. Even better value can be had if you trade up to the Orlando RF (£6.99) range comprising a juicy Cabernet and a medium-bodied Chardonnay, both with just enough oak. St Hilary Chardonnay 1991 (QW £9.99) is jam- packed with ripe fruit, pure gold and exploding with flavour but I always find it difficult to match it with a sufficiently flavoursome dish. St Hugo Coonawara Cabernet Sauvignon 1990 (QW £9.99) is pure essence of blackcur-rants with a minty whiff in classic old-fashioned Coonawarra style. Carrington (£7.99) is a tank-fermented sparkler, a style pioneered by Orlando, which is aged on its yeasty sediment. The result is a sur-prisingly complex wine in the white and a pleasantly frivolous pink with a touch of off-dry strawberry fruit.

Peter Lehman is a folk hero amongst the growers of the Barossa Valley and it's delightful to drink a glass of cool Chardonnay at his weigh-station and watch the sun go down over the vines. But the wines? Perfectly decent wines, of course, and they are followed religiously by the UK chain, Oddbins. But they seem to lack excitement, with the exception of the gluggable and - in Australia at any rate - rather unusual Grenache (£4.99). A conspicuous underachiever at present. Let's hope things change soon, because the potential is there.

Mount Langhi Ghiran produces some of the most exciting wines in Victoria. The Riesling 1993 (SQ £7.49) is the best Australian version on the Irish market and a wine to conjure with. The Shiraz (SQ £8.49) is classic and needs a few years bottle age to become magnificent.

Penfolds is Australia's most distinguished wine name thanks to the mould-breaking and fabulously expensive Grange invented by Max Schubert in the 1950s. It's so intense it makes other top Shiraz wines seem like homeopathic grape juice solution by comparison. Grange 1988 (c. £65) is the currently available vintage and highly sought-after by col-lectors. It will need another fifteen to twenty years before it yields up its best. Koonunga Hill Shiraz/Cabernet 1990 (QW £7.09) is big and solid and therefore typical of the Penfolds style, and Koonunga Hill Semillon/

chardonnay 1991 (QW£7.09) all citrus and smoky. Penfolds used to be a rather lack-lustre performer in white wines but now they are right on form. Consider also the tremendously soft, stylish, oaky and intensely berry-ish Bin 389 (QW £10.29))which spends time in ex-Grange casks. Best value of all, though, is probably the dangerously drinkable Coonawarra Shiraz Bin 128 1991 (QW £7.89). Quinnsworth, incidentally, seems to be the cheapest place to buy these wines though demand always outstrips supply. Rawson's Retreat, red and white, are two value-for-money wines which are so-far available only in the UK.

Rosemount in a sense introduced Ireland to Australian wine when the brand arrived here in the early 1980s. Rosemount Estate Cabernet Sauvignon 1994 (£7.99) is a textbook example of why Australian wine has become so popular. Even more so, the Shiraz 1994 (£7.99) with its taste of blackcurrant fruit pastilles, warm, gentle fruit and elegant, vanilla finish. The Coonawarra Estate Show Reserve Cabernet Sauvignon 1992 (QW £10.99) is even better. It has amazing depth and is one of the few Australian reds I can see getting better with age. Tasting it in Australia I suggested it tasted like a Pauillac from Bordeaux - no mean achievement for a New World wine, especially at the price. There's even a whiff of Chateau Latour about it. Their wine-maker told me that this was not deliberate but frequently mentioned in blind tastings. The whites are equally impressive, particularly the Hunter Valley Show Reserve Chardonnay 1992(£10.99) with its ripe melon and cloves nose and the remarkable Roxburgh Chardonnay 1992 (SQ £21.39) which comes closer in style to top class white Burgundy than any other Australian Chardonnay I've yet tasted. Having had a vertical tasting of Roxburgh, right through from the first 1984, I've no doubt that this wine is currently Australia's finest white - and with significant ageing potential. The 1991 vintage, however, is superb right now.

Rothbury is another Hunter Valley company, founded by the famous Len Evans. I like the fairly simple but spicy Shiraz although it's noticeably lighter than it was some years ago(£6.99) and their rather French Hunter Valley Chardonnay 1989 (£7.99). The Hunter Valley Semillon 1993 needs about fifteen years ageing, whereupon it will yield up its magic - if it's anything like the 1977 I tasted at the winery a couple of years ago. Rothbury seems to be in a state of flux at the moment and they need to address one particular problem: all of their Chardonnays taste, to me, very similar.

Chateau Reynella in McLaren Vale is part of Yalumba. Look out for the gloriously soft, dark, fruity, spicy whopping Basket Press Shiraz and the milder, leaner, mintier Basket Press Cabernet Sauvignon. Stony Hill Chardonnay 1990 is rather old-fashioned in terms of big, buttery structure but the bottle age has tamed it into something very toothsome.

Shaw and Smith Reserve Chardonnay (£9.99) is exclusive to Superquinn and is brilliant in a Burgundian style.

St Hallett has given me considerable pause for thought. Old Block Shiraz is absolutely brilliant, although my first encounter with it left me unimpressed. However, as it happens to be one of Australia's true cult wines, it's virtually impossible to get. There's still some knocking about on the odd restaurant list and it's worth snapping if you're lucky enough to find any. The Chardonnay 1991 (£13.09) is given the handcrafted touch but I don't count it amongst Australia's finest.

Chateau Tahbilk in Victoria make unusual, very traditional wines at very competitive prices. The delicious Marsanne (1992) makes the version from nearby Mitchelton look rather meek and mild by comparison but there's nothing unbalanced about this peachy, honeysuckle-scented, very ripe but crisp, nicely oaked white. The Chardonnay is ripe, buttery, deep gold and opens up nicely at about four years old. The Cabernet Sauvignon 1991 is very dark, almost black but with a surprisingly light touch and soft, discrete tannins while packing a lot of fruit.

EASTERN EUROPE

The first I heard of the Peace Process was on Bulgarian Radio as I wended my way into Melnik, way down near the Greek border. My Bulgarian driver had alarmed me before departure by explaining that the journey would take 'two or three days'; I was pretty sure that he meant hours - but perhaps not. His account of the IRA cease-fire, mainly conveyed in hand gestures correlating almost exactly to dangerous bends, seemed very far-fetched but, happily, correct as it turned out.

So, this part of Bulgaria rather sticks in my mind. Sitting under a walnut tree in the sun eating lamb kebabs with cumin and tomato salad - in a village which has not changed in its essentials for centuries - and drinking the remarkably good local red wine which was served a little cool. It was idyllic.

Now, not all of Bulgaria is quite so picturesque. Russe, on the Danube, looks across to one of Romania's biggest industrial centres and its own 1950s communist architecture is not calculated to raise the flagging spirits. But the local wines are excellent.

It seems only the other day that aspirant Irish wine buffs were cutting their teeth on those good old Bulgarian varietals. It was tough of course. It took a lot of imagination to find hints of plums and fruitcake on a £3.49 Haskovo Merlot and it was quite a while before I got round to tasting a real Pomerol. But the vulgar Bulgars captured the imagination of a generation of wine buffs and ordinary consumers. Then, along came the Australians and we were on the pig's back with fruit flavours that we never knew existed - certainly not at £4.99. Poor old Bulgaria got forgotten, but they are still making some very decent wines.

Mind you, they also make oceans of garbage. I spent a week visiting Bulgarian wineries, eating interminable tomato salads and getting eaten alive by mosquitoes the size of Jack Russells. In some wineries the stuff was amazingly good and very cheap. In others, it was frightful. Asked to comment on behalf of the group of wine writers at one such tasting I summoned up all my powers of Irish doublespeak and told the beaming winemaker that 'good is simply not the word' for his wines.

Happily, Bulgarian Vintners who account for most Bulgarian wine in Ireland, are quite selective about what goes on the shelves. The best value and some of the weirdest blends are in the Country Wines selection. Broadly speaking, the whites still lag behind the reds but there are notable exceptions (see below).

Privatisation is the big current issue and foreign investment is what will determine Bulgaria's ability to keep pace with the rest of the world (or even to catch up in certain respects). You can tell the wineries which are earmarked for privatisation. They are all smartly painted and scrupulously clean - a perfect example being the exemplary one at Stambolovo where they make very decent merlot. The less fortunate wineries vary from the grubby and chaotic to the mildly clean and tidy. A European health and safety inspector would simply not survive the tour.

Amongst the whites, it's the unlikely combination in Muskat and Ugni Blanc Russe (£4.49) that has impressed me most with its grapey freshness. Chardonnay is coming on, the best example to date being Reserve Chardonnay Russe (£4.99). Merlot and Pinot Noir Sliven, (£4.49) is a crazy combination of grapes but delicious and gulpable at a fair price. Cabernet and Merlot Pavlikeni (£4.49) has quite a lot of style in a bordeaux kind of way. Stambolovo Merlot Reserve (£4.99) from a merlot-specialist winery, with its sweet, plum pudding fruit ,spicy vanilla oak and silky finish, is the most impressive Bulgarian I've tasted.

Mehana used to be unspeakably awful - a red and white which bore a passing resemblance to wine. Times have changed, however, and Mehana red is a perfectly decent red wine for glugging purposes, the white very crisp, fruity and, I suspect, based on muscat.

The Bulgarian wine industry is still a great source of foreign currency and so there is a will to make it work. Slowly, they are taking an interest in viticulture as distinct from just wine making and they are using consultants from other wine producing countries, notably Australia. Whether Bulgaria will ever be more than a source of cheap and pleasant wines only time will tell.

HUNGARY

Unlike Bulgaria, Hungary has a fine old tradition of serious winemaking and there indications that this will be an area of major excitement over the next few years. There is substantial foreign investment flowing in, the place is awash with Australian consultants and flying winemakers. Even Piero Antinori and Hugh Johnson have their fingers in various Hungarian pies. But the legacy of the bad old days is proving as difficult to shift as one of those stubborn stains you hear about on detergent commercials.

The great wine of Hungary is, of course, Tokay. During the days of Communism wine was made in rather shabby collective wineries and was all drunk locally. However, the State took a special interest in Tokay and somehow, the tradition was kept alive. Of course, being State-run, standards dropped and there is no doubt that the winemaking became dreadfully sloppy. So much so that the wine was invariably seriously oxidised. A whole generation of officials grew up believing that this was what Tokay should taste of. And when Michel Cazes of Chateau Lynch Bages started making Tokay in his usual meticulous way, the local authorities refused to give it official recognition because it didn't taste sufficiently oxidised!

His Tokay Aszu 5 Puttonyos 1988 (SN £10.60) and Tokay Aszu 6 Puttonyos 1983 (SN £15.60), are remarkably intense, sweet, balanced and smelling of cedarwood and cigar tobacco. And if you want a white wine with a difference you could try Disznoko Furmint 1992 (S £6.95), dry and fairly full, not unlike a pinot gris in fact. There's an intriguing yeastiness - almost beery - when you sniff the drained glass.

The Antinori team from Tuscany produce a commendably exciting and original range of Hungarians which include the Tramini Bataapati (£4.99), a dead ringer for a bone dry, firm-fruited Alsace gewurztraminer. On the nose you get a pungent, spicy whiff of lychees , on the palate it's beautifully ripe with enough - just enough acidity - to make it all rather lively. If this is an indicator of what a high quality producer can do in Hungary at this price, it's a case of watch this space. The other white, Zoldveltini (£4.99) is unusual but very attractive: big, ripe fruit, a bit floral, very distinctive. It screams high-tech, squeaky clean wine making.

The red Kekfrankos (£4.99) is a modern interpretation of a wine that has been around, in rather shaky shape, for yonks (though not available in Ireland). It's a light, cherryish red with a faint whiff of tobacco on the nose and makes a pleasant mouthful, especially at the price. It can take a little chilling and I could imagine it going down well with salmon mayonnaise - but don't hold me to that!

The young Australian-trained winemaker Hugh Ryman is making wine just about everywhere he can but even this much travelled wine producer is very excited about the potential of Hungary. In general his wines lag somewhat behind Antinori's. His Gyongyos (pronounced 'join-gosh') Sauvignon Blanc 1994 (QW/McC £4.99) is quite varietal, with appropriate notes of gooseberries and green leaves. It's crisp and well-balanced but I'm not mad about the touch of residual sugar that seems to boot this decent wine into a rather commercial category. The Chardonnay 1994 (QW/McC £4.99) is less afflicted but equally cleanly made in the modern idiom. It's not bursting with character, though, which is perhaps not surprising at the price. Nevertheless, these wines suggest that Hungary has potential and people like Ryman will get right on top of it eventually.

The Chapel Hill range from Balatonbogar is, I suspect, packaged to look Australian. The Oaked Chardonnay 1994 (£4.99) is not half bad, while the Merlot and Cabernet are fine but seem a bit dilute. Villany Hungarian

Selection Cabernet Sauvignon (£4.49) is not bad but there are similarly priced wines with less tannin and more fruit. Early days yet, one suspects.

ROMANIA

Romania is the Eastern European Country with the closest links to France. There's a very long and not entirely undistinguished tradition of winemaking there but there's no doubt that things went down the tubes during the Ceaucescu era. Romania, strange as it may seem produces some good Pinot Noir. It's not even remotely Burgundian and I have to say that Pinot People in places like Oregon and New Zealand don't need to worry about an Eastern Bloc imitator.

No, Romanian Pinot Noir is very rich, ripe, jammy and you can tell what the grape is. It's big stuff, with a very pronounced nose, clean, full of flavour and reasonably long - which is a lot more than can be said for many £4.99 wines. There's only one on the market, so you can't miss it.

I had a brilliant Cabernet Sauvignon Special Reserve 1985 which had lots of blackcurrant fruit, oodles of spicy American oak, decent structure and a good firm finish. It wasn't a million miles away from a mature cru bourgeois claret - except for its £4.99 price tag. Naturally, it vanished off the supermarket shelves in no time. The current 1986 vintage is not in the same league at all. I suspect slapdash winemaking because it smells, to me at any rate, decidedly strange.

There are several other Romanian Cabernets around and some are in the same mould as the yummy pinot, while others have a rather nasty pong of damp cardboard. The problem here is consistency. You can be very lucky or very unfortunate. The whites, incidentally, are not yet up to much but I reckon that Romania in general is getting better and better. Definitely a country to dip into from time to time.

FRANCE

ALSACE

How come Alsace wines are so unfashionable? Because they come in German-style bottles and have German-sounding names like riesling and gewurztraminer.

Some people actually think Alsace is *in* Germany. Try telling an Alsatian that and you'll get your ankle bitten. Alsace has not had it easy. Separated from Germany by the Rhine and from the rest of France by the Vosges mountains, Alsace has been the subject of many historical disputes. It was taken over by Germany in 1871 and the vineyards were allowed to decline. Returned to France in 1918, the Alsaciennes did their best to get back on track only to be invaded, yet again, by the Germans during the Second World War. While many Alsace natives speak a kind of German dialect, it's not hard to see why they have a very keen sense of Frenchness.

Having said that, the little villages which dot the province are very Germanic in appearance and the food would not disappoint a Teutonic trencherman. Famed for its charcuterie and sauerkraut the Frenchness of the Alsaciennes is best expressed, I believe, in the creamy onion tart that they make better there than anywhere else on the globe. A ripe but dry Pinot Gris with this sweet-but-savoury masterpiece is very heaven. And I'll pass on the boiled sausage with pickled cabbage, thank you very much.

Odd as it may seem, Alsace producers were using varietal labelling (putting the name of the grape on the bottle) long before the Californians ever thought of it. And that tells you a lot about Alsace wines. They are as easy to understand as they are grossly under-rated.

Alsace has very low rainfall and a complex mixture of soils running down the long, narrow strip of territory where vines are grown. Most wines are given a dose of sugar before fermentation to ensure decent alcohol levels. This chaptalisation is practiced to varying degrees throughout France but the Alsace producers are less reticent about admitting to it. They also do it so well that you generally don't notice it.

Alsace grand cru wines come from specific vineyards with lower yields and a higher natural sugar content than the ordinary wines. In general they are more concentrated and some are exceptionally good.

The basic Edelzwicker blend is usually made from Chasselas and Sylvaner. Usually quite dry and simple, they are rarely much to write home about and very little makes it to export markets.
But the most famous Alsace varietal is the chunkily named gewurztraminer. This is one helluva an aromatic grape, redolent of lychees and spice. Low acidity means it's very easy to drink and spiciness means it can cope with relatively mild Indian and Chinese food.

To me, Gewurztraminer makes a perfect aperitif or wine to be drunk without food. It sure has flavour, enough fruit, as a rule, to give a mild suggestion of sweetness in a dry wine, and lots of aroma. I've been much impressed by Hugel's stunningly intense Gewurztraminer Jubilee Reserve Personelle 1986 some of which is still knocking around on restaurant lists. The more modest, softer but nonetheless excellent Turckheim Tradition Gewurztraminer 1992 (McC £8.75) from the first class Turckheim cooperative is a very sound buy.

Alsace Rieslings, on the other hand, tend to be steely, acidic, and a little floral on the nose. When they have a few years' bottle age they tend to develop a hint of 'petrol' on the nose which, despite the associations of the word, is far from unpleasant. Alsace producers revere Riesling and maintain that their best efforts come from this noble grape. Trimbach Riesling 1991 (£8.49) is old enough to have developed the 'petrol' nose with lashings of crisp acidity, good fruit and a bone dry finish. I can think of few better accompaniments to simply-cooked salmon - and none that beat it for sheer value.

Muscat, that grapiest of grapes, is almost always vinified dry in Alsace and is one of my favourites: masses of fragrant grapes on the nose and a bone dry taste. I suppose the relative unpopularity of Alsace wines explains why Muscat is hard to come by but it's worth snapping up if you come across it. The best example I've had in the past few years has been the Muscat d'Alsace Cuvée Reserve Turckheim 1992 (McC £8.99).

Pinot blanc, neutral in many ways, can produce a lovely full, easy, gentle white wine in Alsace and a prime example, in my experience is Hugel's Pinot Blanc Cuvée Les Amours 1991 (McC £7.99)which features as house white in some discerning restaurant lists but is distressingly hard to get hold off in the supermarket or off-licence. Richer and earthier is the Pinot Blanc Schlumberger 1991/1992 (F £8.99).

Pinot Gris, known also as Tokay d'Alsace and, in Italy, as Pinot Grigio, is, for me, the most interesting and challenging of the Alsace varietals. When nice and ripe, but vinified quite dry, it has remarkable complexity, length, depth, interest and a curious, mouth-watering citrusy (grapefruit?) quality. The only readily available example I can think of is Leon Beyer's Tokay Pinot Gris Cuvée Particuliere 1985 (SN £16.70) and, while not cheap, it's well worth seeking out if you want to experience the value-for-money aspect of Alsace. Try this and you'll see why the *cognoscenti* are so keen.

Cremant d'Alsace is the local sparkler, usually made with Pinot Blanc but any variety except the aromatic Gewurztraminer may be used. Dopff au Moulin Cremant d'Alsace (MI £11.95) is very crisp, dry and refreshing and makes a pleasant alternative to other sparklers.

Leon Beyer is regarded as a good producer and, indeed, some older vintages are impressive. However, I believe the quality is in decline.

Dopff au Moulin make excellent wines offering remarkable value and their Riesling 1991 (MI £8.70) is a great introduction. Schoenenburg Riesling Grand Cru 1990 (MI £12.95) is a great buy.

Dopff & Irion have gone through a rather lack-lustre phase but there are signs that they are returning to form.

Theo Faller is one of the top producers and, like Zind-Humbrecht, noted for wines of great finesse and concentration. Not cheap, of course, but like all top Alsace wines they are worth every penny. Available from Searson's.

Hunawihr make sound wines, very fairly priced. Their Pinot Blanc (SN£6.95) is a steal.

Hugel is run by the legendary and larger-than-life Johnny Hugel who has become a kind of unofficial ambassador for the region. He makes outstanding *vendage tardive* and *selection de grains nobles* wines but the more commercial offerings are sometimes less concentrated than his competitors. Very sound, however, and widely available.

Kugler's wines are very modest and simple, but very keenly priced.

Gustave Lorentz is reputed to be a serious producer of value-for-money wines.

Schlumberger's vineyards tend to lie in the warmer South of the the region and include some exceptionally well exposed sites which yield riper fruit. The wines have an impressive depth of flavour but are hard to come by on the retail market. Their *grand cru* wines such as the Gewurztraminer Kessler and Riesling Kitterle are real classics and pretty dear to boot.

Pierre Sparr makes good commercial wines.

Trimbach's house style tends towards the dry and elegant. Very sound wines, widely available. Tokay Pinot Gris Reserve 1992 (£10.69) is simply delicious.

Zind-Humbrecht make some of Alsace's finest wines sometimes with such staggering intensity that they can taste sweet in a ripe vintage. Not cheap, made in small quantities and therefore quite hard to find, they are all stunners. The wholesaler is Colm Brangan (01 821 4052) who can advise on availability which is exclusive, so far, to selected restaurants.

Wolfberger is the biggest cooperative winery in Alsace making light, easy wines which are exclusive to Quinnsworth. However, with really good stuff from other producers easily available at similar prices they have very stiff competition. Nevertheless, the riesling 1994 and Pinot Blanc 1994 are good buys at £6.49.

Gassmann, Gieselbrecht and Kuentz-Bas are all excellent but not available in Ireland.

ANJOU - see Loire

BANDOL
Bandol is generally regarded as being the best Provence wine, almost all of it in the form of big, beefy reds. The big grape here is Mourvedre but there's also some Syrah and Carignan. Pink Bandol is made from Grenache and Cinsault, the white from Bourbelenc, Clairette and Ugni Blanc. Perhaps these rather non-mainstream grape varieties explain why Bandol, in all its forms, make such a pleasant change from the varietal-dominated New World wines which seem to be everywhere these days.

Bandol is not exactly thick on the ground in Ireland but the best example, Domaine Tempier can be found in a few good wine shops. Domaine de Tempier 1990 (McC £14.50) is dark, spicy, full and a bit herby. The herby Domaine Tempier Rose 1990 (SN £10.95) reminds me of that wonderful Provencale smell of wild thyme on the warm wind and is the only wine I know that can tackle globe artichokes. No mean achievement!

Tempier is slowly developing something of a cult following in Dublin ever since it was first clasped to the bosom of a certain coterie of rock stars. Hence the prominent billing it gets in Cooke's Cafe - and, perhaps, the price.

The wines of Mas de la Rouviere (McC/T/G £9.99) are rather more affordable and a good introduction to the regional style: a soft, easy red, a waxy, oily, superb white to go with the herbs and garlic of Provençale fish cookery, and there's a pretty, pungent rosé. Not yet widely distributed but worth asking for.

BANYULS
This is a rarely seen fortified sweet wine made in Roussillon, mainly from Grenache noir. Harvested at the peak of ripeness, the grapes are often half way to turning into raisins and this explains the baked, hot, fruit-cake kind of taste that characterise Domaine de la Rectorie Rimage (McC£7.50). Using a kind of solera system which explains the curious, Madeira-like hint of oxidation, Domaine de la Rectorie con-tains a proportion of 30 year-old wine. A perfect compliment to bitter, dark chocolate and, so they say, not half bad with lobster. The nearest thing to it that most of us have tasted is port. Banyuls Grand Cru Sec Cuvee Joseph Nadal 1983 (SQ/MI £16.49) is aged in wood to produce an extraordinary tawny-coloured wine which looks like amontillado sherry but doesn't have the same nutty taste. Served cool it makes a weird but rather wonderful aperitif. Attractive stuff, but not everybody's glass of Beaumes de Venise.

BARSAC - see Bordeaux

Coteaux d'AIX EN PROVENCE
The top property, Chateau Vignelaure, now in Irish hands, has been nod-ding for years. Hopefully the new regime will put this right because the wine is just not up to snuff at the moment.

Coteaux des BAUX EN PROVENCE
The most exciting property here, and one of the most exciting in Europe,

is Domaine de Trevallon where they make fabulously rich, complex, age-worthy wines that give some of the best clarets a very good run for their money. Drinkable when young, it develops into something really sublime at ten or more years of age. Domaine de Trevallon 1988/89(£15.99) is not only good value, but, I reckon, a very sound investment. The 1983, if you can get it, has reached a peak of perfection with much of the character of a Medoc wine but retaining an elusive suggestion of southern herbs. While far from cheap, it's interesting how a wine of this quality can still offer reasonable value for money by comparison to more famous names.

BEAUJOLAIS

I used to sneer at Beaujolais but I think I'm breaking the habit. One of the first wines I ever drank with proper attention, strange as it may seem, was the Beaujolais Nouveau of 1976 which came from a super-ripe vintage. As a callow youth, I was discovering that red wine could be soft and fruity and highly gluggable. Beaujolais Nouveau is now virtually a thing of the past. Making wines which are designed to be drunk at a few weeks old is an exercise in defying nature and it's not cheap. That's why the only times I'm likely to enjoy this dark purple aberration is in the form of a *pichet* in a modest restaurant somewhere in Paris where it costs about four quid. Not for me the stuff that retails at almost £7 in Irish supermarkets. It's just not worth it.

Beaujolais, at its best, turns the usually rather tough Gamay Noir a Jus Blanc (quite a name for a modest grape) into an aromatic, deep coloured red wine with so little tannin that it can be chilled, and an inviting nose which always suggests to me a cross between over-ripe bananas and Juicy Fruit chewing gum. Carbonic maceration may sound like an unpleasant surgical procedure but it is, in fact, a fermentation technique. This is what delivers chewing gum and bananas. Okay, maybe there's also a touch of raspberries and dark cherries if you're in luck, but its simple, pleasant, one-dimensional stuff.

Basic Beaujolais is usually just that. It's so easy to sell that too many negociants have taken the easy option and are quite content to bottle any old rubbish to meet demand. Wine people are particularly prone to shooting themselves in the foot like this. Just look at the Germans.

I find the best policy is to look for the dearer kind of Beaujolais - the ones with the extra name, or Beaujolais *Crus* if you want to be technical. These are as follows Brouilly, Chenas, Chiroubles, Fleurie, Julienas, Moulin-a-Vent, Morgon, Regnie and St Amour. Fleurie is one of Ireland's most popular restaurant wines - presumably because it sounds pretty and is easy to pronounce. Chiroubles somehow doesn't have quite the same ring, but I can't understand why the romantic-sounding St Amour has not caught on. One wine merchant of my acquaintance considered doing a St Amour promotion for St Valentine's Day using a free condom as the incentive - but he was finally dissuaded by the bemused wine supplier.

Brouilly tends to be big and full, Chiroubles is usually very light, Fleurie just a little bigger, Moulin a Vent is relatively long-lived and can begin to taste of Pinot Noir after a few years in bottle, Morgon at its best can be similar, Regnie is wide and varied and St Amour is rather ordinary. At least, that's how I read them, but the point is that not all Beaujolais is the same.

I like a lightly-chilled Brouilly or a cool, mature Moulin-a-Vent and I know from experience that there are few wines which seem so perfectly at home with a French picnic: some bread, some sausage, a hunk of cheese and a pitcher of cool Beaujolais.

Negociant Beaujolais (that is, wine bought, blended and sold under a merchant's label) tends to be boring but Faiveley is a noble exception. Even their Fleurie tastes interesting. Georges Dubeouf is revered throughout the wine world as the king of Beaujolais but I have to say that I find the Duboeuf house style dominating the wines and making them all taste pretty much the same. I will admit that he produces a decent bottle, though.

The most serious Beaujolais that I've tasted recently, however, are both

Domaine wines which means that they are grown, made and bottled on the one site. These are Morgon Cote du Py 1993, Domaine Savoye (SN £9.75) which shows that a Beaujolais *cru* can be much more than one-dimensional; and the velvet, utterly delicious, gentle Fleurie La Roilette 1994 Vieilles Vignes Andre Metrat (S N£10.40). I'm sure there are more and, now that I'm getting over my prejudice, I reckon I stand a good chance of finding a few. The problem remains, however, of Beaujolais being regarded by most Irish wine merchants as a kind of commodity wine - a wine that will sell no matter how awful it turns out to be.

BERGERAC

Bergerac is not exactly a happening wine spot. It hit the headlines a few years ago when a rather modest local red was discovered in the act of pretending to be Chateau Latour. A number of minor negociants are still doing time. However, there's nothing wrong with Bergerac itself although it is still very much in the shadow of Bordeaux which is not very far away. There are a number of pleasant reds with some Bordeaux character but the one Bergerac with which I've been particularly impressed is Hugh Ryman's white Domaine de Grand Pouget 1994 (QW £4.99), a nice, crisp, grassy style which reflects this young English wine maker's Australian training while retaining local character. He also makes Chateau Haut Peygonthier 1993 (McC £4.99), a soft, easy, Merlot-dominated red with quite a lot of style. Much energy goes into producing an awful local sweet wine which mercifully rarely escapes from the region. I reckon that the future for Bergerac lies in producing claret-style reds at bargain prices. Otherwise they will have to carve out a new identity for themselves.

BONNEZEAUX - see Loire

BORDEAUX

Bordeaux covers a multitude. To some it will mean simple, branded wines like Mouton Cadet or Calvet Reserve. To others it will evoke memories of St Emilion or Pomerol. To the fortunate few it means the fine and expensive classed-growth wines, while to others Bordeaux is the home of the world's most subtle and impressive sweet wines from Sauternes and Barsac. And then there are the dry white wines, ranging from crisp, simple Entre-Deux-Mers to waxy, oak-aged Graves.

I have spent more time in Bordeaux than in any other wine region of the world and I suspect that I have drunk more fine Bordeaux than I have any other serious wine. And I have to say that I love it. Mature claret - that's the traditional wine buff's name for red Bordeaux - certainly features in my definition of heaven. It's impossible to describe, really, how the dark, tannic, closed wine softens over the years and both the smell and the taste seem to acquire layer upon layer of complexity. It's a joy to look at the colour of an old claret, still intense in the centre but changing to a brick red at the edge. Once, when tasting the still glorious Chateau Leoville Barton 1929 I decided, on the basis of the colour, that it was a 1955!

Yes, for me I can imagine no greater wine pleasure than drinking a great old claret. And, on a more mundane level, younger and less posh claret is delicious and surprisingly dependable. Unlike Burgundy, you can find your way around the wines of Bordeaux without constantly seeking directions. You know where you stand.

Every New World winemaker has tried to imitate Bordeaux but even the very best of them have so far failed to hit the bullseye. Some of the most stunning Californian Cabernets can give you a whiff of the legendary Chateaux Latour or Mouton Rothschild but they always give the game away with the ripeness of the fruit. Even in the ripest of Bordeaux vintages the plump fruit is always hemmed in and strapped into a corset by the tannins. So while they come close, the Bordeaux formula eludes them. The New World winemakers may scoff at the notion of *terroir* (essentially, the uniqueness of a particular place in geophysical and climatic terms and what this does to the taste of wine) but Bordeaux is one region, or collection of mini-regions, which seem to suggest that the 'terroirists' have a point.

BORDEAUX: A QUICK TOUR

This is the simplest account of the geography of Bordeaux you are ever likely to get. I'm assuming that you, like me, are more interested in wine than geography. If you want greater detail, try Hugh Johnson's legendary World Atlas of Wine, the new edition of which is an essential companion for the serious wine buff, armchair-bound or otherwise.

Anyway, on the sea side of the Gironde you have the Medoc which is divided into the Haut Medoc to the south and the Bas Medoc to the north. The Haut Medoc contains all of the classified growths, bar one - of which more anon.

Further south you have Graves and the new appellation of Pessac-Leognan.

On the other side of the river you have what are conveniently called the Libournais wines: St Emilion, Pomerol, Lalande de Pomerol, Fronsac, Bourg, Blaye. You may occasionally see wines from the Cotes de Francs. These regions grow mainly Merlot while the rest of Bordeaux, as far as quality wines are concerned, rely more on Cabernet.

In between there is an area producing generally fairly simple wines such as Entre-Deux-Mers (a name thought up by marketing people in the 1960s) and rather vague-sounding appellations like Cotes de Bordeaux and Premieres Cotes de Bordeaux.

A bit further south you find the dessert wine enclaves: Sauternes and Barsac on one side of the Garonne, and the poor but often interesting relations like Cadillac, Monbazillac, Sainte Croix du Mont and Loupiac, on the other. Here the main grapes are Sauvignon Blanc and Semillon and Muscadelle.

It's hardly surprising that the Bordelais have got the hang of the business; wine was being made hereabouts since at least 379AD when the Roman poet Ausonius celebrated the fact in verse. The oldest surviving wine property is Chateau Pape-Clement in Graves which dates from 1305.

The first attempt to put a shape on Bordeaux's pecking order came in 1855 when the top wines were ranked according to the prices which they were fetching. Later, the region was divided into appellations by far the biggest of which is the straight Bordeaux AC in which, incidentally, the area under vine has more than doubled in the past twenty years. Essentially, Bordeaux AC is the lowest rung on the Bordeaux ladder. Any wine made within Bordeaux can call itself Bordeaux AC, provided it meets certain requirements. But Bordeaux wines made in the communes, places like Pauillac or Moulis or Lalande-de-Pomerol will always carry the commune AC rather than the basic Bordeaux one. In other words, Chateau Mouton Rothschild could call itself Bordeaux rather than Pauillac if it wanted to. Mouton Cadet can only call itself Bordeaux.

The classed-growths or *grands crus classés* of 1855 top the red Bordeaux hierarchy at least as far as the Medoc and Haut-Medoc are concerned. Then come the later classifications of wines known as *cru bourgeois* and *cru grand bourgeois*. Then come the properties which belong to no classification at all - the *petits chateaux*. There is a much looser classification in Pomerol and St Emilion while Graves has recently been split in two. The new appellation of Pessac-Leognan includes all the top wines of the region, while the remaining straight Graves AC wines are, with a few exceptions, not in the same league.

A SIMPLE GUIDE TO THE 1855 CLASSIFICATION

Don't be impressed by a label that bears the legend 'Grand Vin de Bordeaux'. It has no recognised meaning whatsoever.

However, if you're drinking a wine from the Haut Medoc (or its designated communes of Pauillac, Margaux, St Estephe, St Julien) and the label says 'Grand Cru Classé', it means quite a lot.

In 1855 the red wines of the Medoc were ranked according to the price they were fetching at the time. The 61 most expensive wines were then named as *grands crus classés* and divided into *crus* or growths.

The first growths are extraordinary wines fetching equally extraordinary prices. They are Chateaux Lafite, Latour, Margaux, Haut Brion (which somehow crept in from Graves) and Mouton Rothschild. This is rock star territory.

The second growths are: Rausan-Segla (Margaux), Rauzan-Gassies (Margaux), Leoville Las Cases, Leoville-Poyferre, Leoville-Barton (all St Julien), Durfort-Vivens (Margaux), Gruaud-Larose (Margaux), Lascombes (Margaux), Brane-Cantenac (Margaux), Pichon-Longueville-Baron (Pauillac), Pichon-Longueville-Comtesse de Lalande (Pauillac), Ducru-Beaucaillou (St Julien), Cos d'Estournel (St Estephe) and Montrose (St Estephe).

The Third growths are: Kirwan (Margaux), d'Issan (Margaux), Lagrange (St Julien), Giscours (Margaux), Malescot St Exuperay, Boyd-Cantenac (Margaux), Cantenac Brown (Margaux), Palmer (Margaux), La Lagune (Haut Medoc), Desmirail (Margaux), Calon-Segur (St Estephe), Ferriere (Margaux), Marquis d'Alesme Becker.

The fourth growths are: St Pierre Sevaistre (St Julien), Talbot (St Julien), Branaire Ducru (St Julien), Duhart-Milon-Rothschild (Pauillac), Pouget (Margaux), La Tour Carnet (Haut Medoc), Lafon Rochet (St Estephe), Beychevelle (St Julien), Prieure-Lichine (Margaux), Marquis de Terme (Margaux).

Fifth growths are: Pontet Canet (Pauillac), Batailley (Pauillac), Haut Batailley (Pauillac), Grand Puy Lacoste (Pauillac), Grand-Puy-Ducasse (Pauillac), Lynch Bages (Pauillac), Lynch Moussas (Pauillac), Dauzac (Margaux), Mouton Baronne Philippe Pauillac), du Tertre (Margaux), Haut Bages (Pauillac), Pedesclaux (Pauillac), Belgrave (Haut Medoc), Camensac (Haut Medoc), Cos Labory (St Estephe), Clerc Milon (Pauillac), Croizet-Bages (Pauillac), Cantemerle (Haut Medoc).

Of course, times have changed since 1855 and some wines should be promoted (Palmer and Lynch Bages certainly, Grand Puy Lacoste probably) while others should be demoted or kicked out (Marquis d'Alesme

Becker and Croizet-bages for example, on present form at any rate).

And of course, there are several wines which now equal many classed growths in quality and they should really be included - Chasse Spleen, Lanessan, Potensac, d'Angludet all spring to mind.

Bordeaux Vintages
Vintages are important, so let's have a quick look at how they have been. It's hard to generalise - so, if in doubt, consult a wine merchant who knows his or her onions. These comments largely apply to the better wines. For example, Chateau Lynch Bages 1987 (MW £19.50) is superb at eight years old. A petit chateau of the same vintage would be very far down the tubes by now.

1995: Long, warm, dry summer, healthy grapes and good conditions at harvest time would suggest that these wines will be highly satis-factory, possibly even great.

1994: Very warm, dry summer means that the fruit was in great shape by harvest time but then the heavens opened. Everybody wants this to be a great vintage, particularly the Bordeaux wine trade but I'm gobsmacked at Robert Parker, the American wine guru, comparing the 1994s to the very fine 1970s. This is wishful thinking if ever I saw it. It's too early to say, but these wines look to me a little like the 1981s with most wines perfectly decent for the medium haul, a few absolute gems (L'Angelus is magical) but not justifying large scale dancing in the streets.

1993: A disappointing vintage, wines lacking concentration, but some of the better properties made pleasant wines for early drinking. Not unlike the 1991s and, similarly, not for the long haul. Cheaper wines pleasant enough but most of them lacking pzazz.

1992: I am told that there are exceptions but I've yet to find them. Weak, watery, dull wines in general. A washout.

1991: Not nearly as poor as some people make out - some of the great names made good early-maturing wines. The best of the 1991's are peaking around now, often offering a cut-price opportunity to get hold of a ready-to-drink *grand cru.*

1990: Big, fat, well-structured wines. The big names will need at least five years to open up.

1989: I reckon that the 1989s and the 1990s are very similar - but the 1989s seem to have a more conventional tannic structure. For laying down, I'd hedge my bets and use both years.

1988: A good vintage but the best wines have plenty of tannin and need time to soften If you like your claret a little lean and savoury - the classic style, in other words - this is a vintage well worth cellaring.

1987: A light vintage with the more modest wines heading for oblivion by now if they have not already arrived there. The best wines are drinking well now - Chateau Leoville Barton is light, elegant and utterly charming. Not for keeping.

1986: A very good but rather tannic vintage for the dearer wines. The best wines are still a bit hard but more modest wines are opening up nicely.

1985: Big soft wines, in general all drinking well by now.

1984: A washout. Hard, charmless. Forget it.

1983: Overshadowed by the whopping 1982s and starting to drink beautifully - but the very best need a few more years.

1982: Big, luscious, opulent and, more importantly, fashionable and expensive. The best wines will keep for at least another ten years but all are dangerously easy to drink now. Cheaper wines are getting tired.

1981: A mixed vintage - *caveat emptor.* Most top wines now drinking, many in a slow, elegant decline.

1980: Never good, should be forgotten.

BUYING CLARET

First, the bad news. We've had such a run of poor vintages over the past few years that stocks of pleasant, well-made affordable claret are running very low. This is not a good time to be getting into claret, unless you are looking at buying the 1994s and 1995s *en primeur* (before they are bottled) but you will have to talk to a serious wine merchant about this (Searson's and Findlater's have offers) and be very patient while your wines come around. However, there are some opportunities to taste good wines without breaking the bank - see below.

Most cheaper clarets are dominated by soft, easy-drinking Merlot. The same goes for the brands like Mouton Cadet, Michel Lynch, and Calvet Reserve (£6.99-7.49). Are the big brand clarets worth it? In good vintages they're usually dependable and pleasant. But in a vintage like 1992, for example, there was so little decent stuff around you can be sure that very little of it got into the big brand bottles. The cheaper clarets which Quinnsworth always seem to have strike me as being rather more exciting, and frequently better value.

Your best introduction to proper claret might well be Sirius, a straight Bordeaux AC wine which has been given the full treatment by Peter Sichel of the legendary Chateaux Palmer and Angludet. Sirius 1988 (£7.99) is largely Merlot, has had time in oak and is now at a peak of soft, velvety maturity. This seductive Merlot-dominated wine is very much in a Pomerol or St Emilion style, but at rather less than half what you can expect to pay for these famous names. It's hard to know how Sirius will perform in lighter, less successful vintages but Sichel really knows what he's doing.

Chateau Meaume 1992 (£7.50) is a perfectly pleasant wine and not half bad for this atrocious vintage but the reason I mention it is to put you on your mettle. Watch out for the 1993 which I expect will be a great deal better. Alan Johnson-Hill, once a financier in Hong Kong, realised his dream of being a *vigneron* when he acquired this undistinguished property in 1980. It is now synonymous with honest, value-for-money claret, again with a high Merlot content and a big, ripe, luscious quality in vintages like 1990. It's definitely one of the best all rounder in Bordeaux and it's no dearer, really, than the big brands.

If you want affordable claret from older, better vintages at the moment, you will have to make an effort. The supermarkets can't find enough of the stuff, so you must resort to specialists like Searson's in Dublin or the Merchant's Wine Club in Galway. Chateau Latour Saint Bonnet 1989 (SN £8.80) is deliciously mature but will hold another few years, while Chateau Lanessan 1988 (SN £10.35) is a steal: classic claret in a grand cru style, still quite tannic but a great food wine. Chateau Canon Mouiex 1990 (SN £12.70) from Canon-Fronsac is bursting with ripe fruit, ready to drink and puts many a St Emilion in the shade. Chateau Dalem 1990 (£10.50) is in the same mould. Chateau Potensac 1988 (MW £12.50) is a taut, aristocratic wine with a top dressing of really generous fruit. Chateau Suau Cuvee Prestige Premieres Cotes de Bordeaux 1990 (PM) is everything that a reasonably-priced claret should be: soft, presumably because there's a lot of ripe Merlot in there, rich and quite silky on the palate and with a decent, lengthy finish. At £74 a dozen, plus the dreaded VAT at 21%, this is a very pleasant buy. Chateau de France 1990 (MO/DV £11.99) is a very attractive Graves from Pessac-Leognan with the typical tobacco-scented nose that spells good Graves.

However, things being as they are, you will have more choice if you're prepared to trade up a bit. Chateau d'Angludet 1989 (SN £16.70), for example, will give you not only grand cru quality but quite a lot of maturity and complexity too. Chateau Grand Puy Ducasse 1990 (MW £16.50) is a real grand cru from Pauillac. Its blackcurrant fruit and stylish structure make it an exceptionally good buy.

A DRY WHITE BORDEAUX SELECTION

To most people, dry white Bordeaux brings back unspeakable memories of tired, oxidised, flabby stuff that you would be reluctant to pour down the sink for fear of what it might do the local environment. But times have changed and while there's still too much of the old-fashioned gunge around, there's also a whole new generation of bright, light, crisp, zingy white wines around - even from Entre-Deux-Mers the formerly rather lack-lustre appellation whose name was invented by advertising executives in the 1960s.

Chateau Bonnet (£7.50), made by the Lurton family, is always dependable: fresh, crisp, clean and reasonably characterful. In restaurants you will sometimes get the posh version which has had some contact with oak. Chateau La Freynelle 1994 (£6.75) is as fresh as a daisy with a bone dry sauvignon zing. Chateau Pichon Bellevue 1994 (WD £6.50) - this is from the modest appellation of Graves de Vayres but the wine is exciting: lots of well balanced fruit, a crisp, zesty sauvignon nose and it puts many a Sancerre to shame. Chateau de Sours 1994 (MI £8.90) a delicious Bordeaux Superieur, belying its modest appellation, with fresh, ripe fruit, clean, balanced, long and stylish. It's made by Esmé Johnson, founder of the Majestic Wine chain in the UK and is a prime example of where Bordeaux white wines are heading.

Trading up you get into serious territory with Chateau de Thieuley: Cuvee Francis Courselle 1993 (WD £9.12), handcrafted by a passionate winemaker. Long, elegant, oak-aged to perfection, this puts quite a few white Graves to shame. I can't name a single white Burgundy that delivers this much at the price. But if you want to put white Burgundy firmly in the shade, try Chateau La Tour Martillac 1990 (SN £18.50) from Pessac-Leognan in Graves, a superb complex, deep, fabulously intense yet subtle, stylish, elegant white wine with aristocratic fruit, so much French oak that would sink a lesser wine and such sheer elegance that makes me wonder why people pay over twice the price for Corton Charlemagne. And it's going to get even better.

A Sweet White Bordeaux Selection:
The great sweet wines of Bordeaux are, I believe, the best dessert wines in the world. Why? Because like all good sweet wines they achieve a perfect balance between sweetness and acidity and because they manage to maintain a light, almost delicate texture combined with phenomenally concentrated and complex tastes ranging from butterscotch to toasted hazelnuts to citrus fruit. And they can age. Because of their high sugar and acid content, the best Sauternes and Barsac can live for decades. I recently shared a bottle of Chateau Climens 1959 which was only just darkening a little, turning from a pale lemon to something approaching gold. It was so youthful I have no doubt that it will quite magnificent at fifty or even seventy years old.

Of course there's a great prejudice against sweet wines probably based on the fact that most people associate them with gruesome, cheap German wines and have never tasted the great ones. People who are recent recruits to what you might call serious wine often regard dessert wines as rather naff. It's probably embarrassment at being reminded of the days when the height of sophistication for them was a steak and black forest gateau accompanied by a bottle of Liebfraumilch. Well, they don't know what they're missing.

Sweet wines in general went out of fashion for a while and the great wines of Bordeaux, with only a couple of exceptions, were selling amazingly cheaply. But people have realised how wonderful they are, demand is soaring and so have the prices. They have never been cheap to make, of course. The grapes are allowed to become super-ripe which means that yields are tiny. In years when the noble rot strikes (not to be confused with the ignoble grey rot) the wines are even more concentrated. This is because the fungus makes the grape skins more permeable, allowing more evaporation and thus concentrating sugar levels within. Is it any wonder that these wines have been called liquid gold?

Yquem, of course, is the ultimate, selling for hundreds - sometimes thousands - of pounds per bottle. It's sister estate, Chateau de Fargues, makes a very similar and rather cheaper wine of which the 1981 vintage occasionally crops up on wine lists. Chateaux Coutet, Rieussec, Sudiraut, Climens, Nairac and La Tour Blanche are all great names and worth considering. The 1990 vintage, by the way, is a stunner and the wines need time (although they are very, very palatable now). Good Sauternes and Barsac cost around £20 a bottle at their cheapest. Chateau Coutet 1981 (O'B 19.95) is a good wine in a modest vintage and is quite mature. Chateau de la Chartreuse 1988 (QW £14.99) is a snip and needs time.

There is, of course, an alternative. Some excellent sweet wines are made across the river from Sauternes and Barsac in the commune of Loupiac. The best wines have a very similar style, structure and flavour but don't quite achieve the same kind of weight in the mouth. Try Chateau de Ricaud, if you can find it, traditionally regarded as the leading property or, even better, Chateau Loupiac Gaudiet 1991 (SN £12.75) which has a lot of posh Sauternes character and a similar kind of weight even in this lightish vintage. This is remarkable value and you can also have a half bottle (SN£6.95). The 1990, still on some restaurant lists, is a serious Sauternes challenger.

Other Bordeaux stickies include Saint Croix du Mont which I always find rather dilute and crude, Monbazillac which I actively dislike for its cloying barley sugar sweetness and lack of balancing acidity, Cadillac and the rarely seen but occasionally very pleasant Cerons.

If you have never experienced a good Bordeaux sweetie with a chunk of salty, tangy Roquefort cheese, you have missed one of the great taste and texture combinations ever devised.

BURGUNDY

Burgundy, in terms of wine, stretches from Dijon southwards almost as far as Lyon. The first leg of the journey comprises a thirty mile hilly ridge, running from Marsannay to Santenay, known as the Cote d'Or; this is the heart of Burgundy. It's the home of the great names like Gevrey-Chambertin, Corton, Nuits Saint Georges and so forth. The northern half of the Cote d'Or is called the Cotes de Nuits, the southern half is known as the Cotes de Beaune. Further south you have the Cote Challonaise which includes the less well-known Mercurey, Givry, Rully and Montagny. Further south again comes the Maconnais which includes Macon, St Veran, Pouilly-Fuisse and Pouilly-Vinzelles. And then you have Beaujolais which produces radically different wines from different grape varieties and so I don't regard it as being Burgundy in the same sense as the Pinot Noir and Chardonnay areas mentioned above. Just to complicate matters a little further, Chablis is off on its own, a little to the north-west of Burgundy proper.

The classification of Burgundy is relatively simple. The Grands Crus are all perfectly sited. The Premiers Crus are also well-sited, while the straight village wines which carry just the local name and no further qualification come, if you like, from the best of inferior Premiers Cru areas which are not deemed worthy of the classification. Particularly poor spots produce wine which can only be called Bourgogne Rouge. Did I say relatively simple? *Relatively.*

RED BURGUNDY

Burgundy can be the most expensive mistake that a wine buff ever makes - with the possible exception of forgetting the vintage chart and snapping up a case of Mouton Rothschild 1963. The latter is completely undrinkable; the former too often leaves you with a strong sense of having been mugged.

Why, oh why? (To borrow a phrase from Paul, as distinct from Hugh, Johnson.) Well, Burgundy is very different from Bordeaux. There are lots and lots of growers and myriad tiny holdings, often as small as a single row of vines. In certain respects there is a sense of quiet chaos about Burgundy. And, of course, the wines are very fashionable - and, in fact, they don't produce very much of the stuff. As a result, they are dear and unpredictable.

To say that Pinot Noir flourishes in Burgundy is a little misleading. This is as far north as you can make decent red wine - but given the vagaries of the marginal climate you can only really expect to make good stuff once in every three years. I reckon the fact that the vine has to struggle a bit, combined with varying *terroir* makes Burgundy, at its best, so deliciously complex. And some of the properties are so tiny you worry about destroying a work of art in a few gulps. A very posh Bordeaux chateau could produce 20,000 cases a year. A Burgundian establishment at the same quality level could be making only two or three hundred cases.

In Burgundy, as nowhere else, you really need to know what you're looking for. And you need a fairly fat wallet if you want to experience the region at its best. There's a lot of over-priced, lean, mean, dull and boring Burgundy around. And when I say over-priced, I mean daylight robbery.

Because rich wine consumers, just like everyone else, find Bordeaux easier to understand, you will find less tip-top Burgundy on the market than you might expect. Most of what we get here is negociant wine and some negociants, of course, have domaines (or vineyards) of their own. Here, I'm concentrating on negociant wines simply because that's what you're mostly likely to encounter. If you want to seek out the very serious stuff, talk to merchants like Findlater's, Searson's and Brangan's. There is plenty of good stuff about, as well as an ocean of complete dross. Is there a simple rule of thumb to help you steer a safe course? Well, in a way, yes.

Always go for a shipper you can trust and - the two that always spring to mind are Faiveley and Louis Jadot. Drouhin, Jaffelin, Louis Latour, Leroy, Moillard, Rodet, Ropiteau, Remoissenet and Charles Vienot are all names that command respect, and you won't go far wrong with them. Some big names are not as good as they might be - Chanson, Reine Pedauque and Lupe Cholet are quite poor. Laboure-Roi, Mommessin and Bouchard Pere et Fils can be variable. Clair-Daü, Dauvissat, Dujac, Rossignol, Roty, Mugneret, Rion, Marquis de Laguiche, Grivot and, for the ultimate in white burgundy, Domaine Leflaive, are all names that I associate with very happy, if rather expensive Burgundy experiences.

There are few other regions in the wine world - perhaps only Oregon and a few very specific *terroirs* in Australia- where Pinot Noir comes even within shouting distance of good red Burgundy. They talk of these wines showing 'the iron fist in the velvet glove' and whoever first dreamed up that notion got it just right. One of the best introductions to red burgundy is Jadot's glorious Bourgogne Rouge Clos des Jacobins 1988 (£10) which gives you real Burgundy Pinot Noir taste down to the cherries and whiff of what is politely called 'farmyard'. This is real Burgundy, with complexity and length at the kind of price level where competitors get spat out in horror. Charles Vienot's Bourgogne Pinot Noir 1993 (SQ £5.89) is very ripe, full and attractive. It seems light on varietal character and heavy on fruit but excellent value. Rully Rouge 1993 Charles Vienot (SQ£8.79) is similarly fleshy but distinctly Pinot and so light on tannin that it can be drunk cool.

The particularly elegant Savigny Les Beaune Premier Cru Les Lavieres 1992 Charles Vienot (SQ£8.99) and the rather simpler Fixin 1991 Jaffelin (F£9.90) are both excellent examples of how some of the lesser apellations can offer real Burgundian Pinot Noir style without costing a fortune.

I'm not old enough to have tasted, consciously at least, what people now call old-fashioned red Burgundy but I have an idea that Charles Vienot's Monthelie 1990 (SQ£9.99) will satisfy even the most curmudgeonly old buffer. It has great colour, a wealth of opulent, almost New World fruit and a distinctive Pinot Noir nose overlaid with a discreet hint of vanilla-like French oak.

Faiveley's superb Cote de Beaune Villages 1990 (£12.50) is a relatively affordable textbook 'iron fist in the velvet glove' red Burgundy, with delicacy, complexity, length and a very moreish kind of taste. Vosne Romanee Faiveley 1er Cru Les Chaumes 1990 is a very great wine which needs time to become glorious. Like all of Faiveley's domaine wines, it is rigorously traditional and unfiltered. It would be wonderful to be able to put away a few bottles for five or six years. Jadot's Vosne Romanee 1989 (£25) is not a single vineyard wine like Faiveley's but it's both serious and approachable with lots of ripe Pinot Noir fruit and a whiff of violets and truffles - just like they say in the textbooks. And yes, it has an earthy, farmyardy nose too.

WHITE BURGUNDY

It's in Burgundy that the now ubiquitous Chardonnay grape gets closer to vinous perfection than anywhere else. (It can also yield complete dross, of course). In the right hands it produces, to my mind, quite simply the best white wines in the world with tremendous fruit and complexity.

It seems that Elizabeth David, the great food writer, was not as forbidding a companion as one might have thought and that she liked nothing more than to sit chatting in her kitchen over a glass of Chablis. This, I feel, tells you something about her. Firstly that she had made enough money not to worry about the then grossly inflated price of Chablis (she died in the 1980s), and secondly, that she knew exactly what to do with Chablis: drink it casually in the kitchen.

Chablis is a simple wine with a distinctive taste and we need not go into the details of kimmeridgian limestone to understand that. There are some few examples of the wine that fall into the serious stuff league, but let's consider the basic model *sans* go-faster-stripes. It's a simple white wine with a keen edge, a whiff of Chardonnay and, ideally, a nice fresh tang to it.

Basic Chablis is pretty basic wine and so it's good to see some realistic pricing over the last few years. In cheaper wines, look for crisp, lively acidity and a cleansing freshness. Dearer wines should show signs of honeyed fruit, perhaps a touch of flintiness and some complexity. Chablis 1994 Labouré-Roi (QW £8.99) is a very attractive example - but the *premier cru* version, however, is, oddly, not as good. Chablis 1994 Charles Vienot (SQ £8.99) is pleasant, simple wine that is textbook Chablis - with its steely character coming through loud and clear. Names worth looking for include Laroche, Long-Depaquit, Ravenneau, Dauvissat and Fevre. Moreau wines are good and well-priced; the cooperative of La Chablisienne offers very good value.

Charles Vienot's Rully Blanc 1993 (SQ £7.49) has that distinctive, classy, buttery Chardonnay fruit and a touch of stylish, rather toasty, French oak. Elegant and vaguely reminiscent of Meursault this is a welcome reminder that white Burgundy can be heavenly and affordable at the same time.

Up the price scale a little comes Jadot's Auxey Duresses 1990 from the estate of the wonderfully-named Duc de Magenta, a MacMahon. Auxey Duresses is one of Burgundy's less posh bits but the Duc's wines are splendid, particularly the buttery, stylish white 1990 which is serious burgundy for £15.99

Meursault is very posh white Burgundy. I often wonder how often it's drunk by people who actually like the taste of the wine as distinct from the name on the label. Jadot's unctuous and fully mature Meursault Blagny 1986 (£25) is superb and shows just how great Chardonnay can be in its natural home. Nothing from Australia or California can touch it for sheer style, class, subtlety and complexity. At the price, perhaps just as well.

BUZET
An AC for big, peppery reds which was rescued from obscurity by the UK supermarket chain, Sainsbury. After a brief appearance in Quinnsworth it disappeared due to lack of interest. Anybody seen it around?

CAHORS
This is probably the most traditional, classic region of production in the south-west. Traditionally known as the 'black wines of Cahors' they sure have colour and are based mainly on Malbec, or Auxerrois as it's known round here. Chateau de Chambert, Clos Triguedina and Chateau de Haute-Serre are amongst the very best but are mainly confined to restaurants. Retail prices range from £8-11.

CHAMPAGNE

Champagne is still seen as the ultimate wine of celebration. Auberon Waugh has suggested that one reason why it is not liked by more people is because we are often forced to drink it, lukewarm out of shallow glass saucers in the middle of the afternoon. Mind you, not many weddings run to Champagne these days when there's so much good sparkling wine about at less than half the price. Some are barely distinguishable from what the Champenois persist in regarding as the real thing, and anyway most people will never tell the difference between Codorniu and Krug, simply because they drink neither of them on a regular basis.

Champagne is recovering from a particularly bad patch. With vast, yuppie-driven consumption in the 1980s, we were expected to pay silly money for green, nasty acidic wines and be grateful for it. Things have improved and we are now expected to pay equally silly money for something much more drinkable. You can have a bottle of complex, delicious, hand-crafted claret for the same price as a non-vintage Champagne from one of the big names. I know which way I would jump if I had to make the choice.

Leaving price aside - always a difficult thing to do - Champagne can be a delightful wine. The best are indeed as complex as some of the great still white wines. As an aperitif, it's unequalled. When times are good, I try to keep a few half bottles for the odd occasion on which I want to have an elegant reviver before dinner.

Madame Lily Bollinger was one of the great names in Champagne and she once described her approach to consuming it in the following terms. 'I drink it when I am happy and when I am sad,' she said. 'Sometimes I drink it when I am alone. When I have company, I consider it obligatory. I trifle with it when I'm not hungry and drink it when I am. Otherwise I never touch it - unless I'm thirsty.' I like her style.

Someone asked me recently to name my favourite champagne. It was a tough one. It's not unlike being asked to name your favourite Ferrari or your favourite garden or your favourite city. There's pretty stiff competition. However, after lengthy consideration, assisted by the pint of Guinness around which this conversation was taking place, I plumped for Bollinger because of what I call its complexity. Far too many Champagnes are one-dimensional, green, acidic monsters. I don't happen to like sour fizzy wine, just as I'm not inclined to drink Andrews Liver Salts for pleasure.

Bollinger continues to produce big, rich, biscuity Champagnes with a wholesome yeastiness about them. Their basic non-vintage style puts many other houses to shame, including the widely-distributed but deadly dull Mumm whose Napa Valley sparkler from California is, ironically, one of the great sparkling wines - at less than half the price. The ultimate Bollinger is the RD, which stands for 'recently disgorged'. This means that the wine has been aged on its yeasty lees sediment in the bottle and has taken on a very pronounced and complex character. The current Bollinger RD 1982 is one of the greatest Champagnes I've ever tasted. And so it should be at £70 a bottle.

Krug makes outstanding Champagne with amazing length and both the vintage and the very consistent blended Grande Cuvee cost well over £60 a bottle. There's no 'cheap' version for a mere £30. Krug is magnificent, big, assertive yet subtle and delicate at the same time.

Dom Perignon is very good. I like its light, lacy texture and its remarkable delicacy. But I can't say I like its afficionados. I'm sure there are honourable exceptions but there seems to be a striking correlation between DP, vulgar money and the dropping of names which are manifestly *au desous de son gare*. But I'll very gladly drink the stuff. Basic Moet et Chandon is much better value and now firmly re-established as a fine Champagne after a few years in the doldrums, as is the shamefully underrated Ruinart from the same stable.

Roederer Cristal is superb, the champagne of the Czar's and all that. It needs at least a decade to open up and when young is closed, dull and tight. Old Cristal is one of the most sublime wine experiences you can have but as a rule it's drunk well before it reaches the age of consent by people who know no better. 'Ordinary' vintage Roederer, it has to be said, is almost as good if you give it time in bottle.

Really smart Champagnes, of course, are not in the Big Name territory. The cognoscenti will drink Deutz, Gosset, Philloponat and Salon le Mesnil and know that they are not only consuming the finest Champagnes but getting as close to value-for-money as the unreal world of Epernay and Reims will permit.

The style of Pommery, now back with Mitchell's after an absence of some 70 years, is broad, 'biscuity' and rather nearer the Veuve Clicquot or Bollinger end of the spectrum than Laurent Perrier. The vintage and NV wines are good buys and the flagship Cuvée Louise Pommery is superb.

The little-known but excellent Billecart-Salmon wines are now to be found on the odd discerning wine list. The rosé is particularly successful.

Charles Heidsieck produces a nice, big style with lots of Pinot character, but Piper-Heidsieck seems to me to be one of the poorest of the famous names. Taittinger deserves to be better known and both Pol Roger and Perrier Jouet produce excellent wines. I've never had a disappointing bottle from any of them.

My taste in Champagne runs more to the big style and there is great consistency to Veuve Clicquot with its distinctive orange label. The flagship La Grande Dame (c £55) is under-rated by the Dom Perignon guzzlers whom I suspect eschew it because they don't regard the label as a fashion accessory.

Finally, some people seem to think that vintage Champagne is intrinsically better than the non-vintage blend. This is not always the case at all. Don't forget that vintage Champagne needs time to develop. It should not be drunk at less than five years old unless you want to waste your money. Even non-vintage Champagne will get better after a few years in the bottle. One of my happiest Champagne memories is of drinking Bollinger NV which had spent the better part of a decade in the cellar.

Lanson's house style is rather green and characterless and there is much room for improvement and Laurent Perrier seems harsher and less ripe than it has been. Perhaps it's a case of Homer nodding, but I fear it reflects the fact that this grand old house is no longer in family ownership.

Amongst cheaper Champagnes, Superquinn's Raymond de Belval (SQ £13.59) gets top marks for value. You will find Henri Goutourbe and Paul Herard as good 'house' Champagnes in decent restaurants.

Mme Bollinger remains the greatest authority on when to drink Champagne but there is still the question of *how?* Just observe two golden rules and you won't be disappointed. Don't be tempted to over-chill the wine - it's best drunk cool rather than cold if you want to actually taste it. And never, ever, ever use those ghastly glass saucers which are said to have been moulded around a certain part of Catherine the Great's anatomy. Use tall, slim, tapering Champagne flutes which will hold the fizz much better and allow you to enjoy the visual aspect of Champagne - the tiny bubbles. The tinier the bubble, the better the wine. And, by the way, always rinse the glasses meticulously. The slightest residue of detergent will turn your expensive little treat into a very flat wine in seconds.

CORBIERES
Corbieres is way down in the south of France. It's only a step from both Narbonne and the Med and, just as you would expect, the hillsides are covered with wild thyme and rosemary wherever the vines have not been planted. It's not a region well-known for fine wines.

Corbieres has been less successful than Minervois in shaking off its reputation as one of the natural homes of rotgut but it has the same amount of potential as any of the other emerging wine regions of southern France. There's a handful of properties leading the way, of course, and Chateau Haut Gleon £10) is one to conjure with. I've known its massive, hard, tannic red for some years now. It's the kind of wine that needs opening the day before you drink it but once that evolution of flavour starts you know you're dealing with something special. If you like your wines so big it seems like they've overdosed on anabolic steroids, this is one for you. Provided you like your tannins firm and stiff-upper-lipped.

Chateau Haut Gleon, however, also makes a couple of thousand cases of white wine. This is great stuff and a welcome relief from the tidal wave of Chardonnay and Sauvignon Blanc which threatens to drown the Irish palate. And it's so far from these classic if over-exposed varietals that it's made from the traditionally rather unexciting Bourboulenc and the...er...traditionally rather unexciting Grenache Blanc (described, I see, by one rather snooty French authority as being 'd'origine Espagnole').

But at Chateau Haut Gleon they manage to turn out a wine with tons of fruit, crisp, racy acidity, plenty of length and a flavour which seems to involve lime, toasted hazelnuts, a faint whiff of pineapple and a chaste oaky peck on the cheek. The exceptionally dry, vaguely astringent finish makes it a delightful companion for seafood. It worked very well for me with a dish of crab claws and green mayonnaise. Chateau Haut Gleon Blanc 1993 (£10.50 DV/MO) is one of the most refreshingly different white wines I've enjoyed over the past year or so.

The brilliant oak-aged Chateau Saint Auriol 1993 (S N£6.85) is probably the best value in Corbieres with its spicy, peppery nose and masses of chewy fruit - and quite an improvement on the 1992. Chateau La Voulte-Gasparets 1989 (SN £7.45) is very big, a little hard, but underlines a rigorous pursuit of quality which one doesn't usually associate with this neck of the woods. Much as I like the alleged ultimate wine of the region, Chateau de Lastours 1989, Cuvee Simone Deshamps (McC £9.50) I don't think it justifies such a whopping price tag.

Domaine du Grand Crès, Corbieres 1991 (WD£6.69) has a very posh pedigree, being made by Hervé Leferrer, the former cellar-master at ultra-posh Domaine de la Romanée-Conti in Burgundy and given some time in oak casks bought secondhand from Chateau Margaux. Actually, here is a Corbieres that can take a bit of age and I reckon it will become even more elegant with two more years or so in bottle. There is a certain suggestion of the iron fist in the velvet glove and sure it's not off the stones the wine licked it.

More traditional but really packed with fruit is the Chateau Cascadais, Corbieres 1992 (WD£6.40)

Cotes de DURAS

Supposedly a good source of simple Sauvignon whites, but it lives in the shadow of nearby Bordeaux. Hugh Ryman's Domaine de Malardeau 1994 Sauvignon Blanc (McC £4.99) is a cracker. There are some pleasant, fresh cheap sweet wines made for local consumption and which are worth asking for if you're ever passing through.

FITOU

Fitou, which is part of Languedoc, is cut in half by Corbieres. The part nearer the sea is said to produce the best wines, but some of the stuff emanating from the hillier, inland part seems fine to me. In recent years the grip of the cooperatives has loosened and some, such as Mont Tauch, have helped to lead the way to quality. Fitou at its best can be delicious - full, dark and peppery. Fitou Resplandy 1990 (£4.99) is all gone now but was a case in point. The 1991 vintage is simply not in the same league but the 1993 which is becoming available is a move in the right direction. The light but wonderfully herbaceous Fitou 1991 Marks & Spencer (MS £4.99) from the Mont Tauch coop is one of the best buys at the price. It's available elsewhere under the Mont Tauch label for a little extra. This cooperative produces splendid wines, none more so than the enormous and highly serious Terroirs de Tuchan (£10), a kind of *tete de cuvee* with attitude. Peppery, spicy, blackberryish it has great length, ripe tannins and quite a few years to go although it's drinking superbly now.

From the same stable comes the very stylish Fitou 1989/91 Chateau de Segure (£6.99) - one of my regular house wines. The lesser wines have a fair amount of Carignan, a grape which lacks oomph. But now there are lots of plantings of Grenache, Syrah and Mourvedre which means that Fitou will undoubtedly get better.

Cotes du FRONTONNAIS

Soft, jammy and very smooth reds when at their best - from north of Toulouse. They are unusual in being made from the local grape variety, Negrette - but Syrah and Cabernet also feature. Try Chateau Bellevue La Foret (£5.99) as a pleasant, easy, uncomplicated red. There is a modest local white wine, Vin de Pays du Comte Toulosan.

Cotes de GASCOGNE

Now becoming firmly established as a source of cheap, fresh, attractive white wines and, to a large extent led out of obscurity by the brilliant Plaimont cooperative. Colombelle 1993 Plaimont (F £4.99) is dry, delicious and full of zing. Cotes de Gascogne 1993 Plaimont (£4.79) is a well-made, attractive, easy-drinking white at a decent price. Domaine du Rey 1992 (SN £4.99) is a light, fresh white with a tang of green gooseberries - but it contains no Sauvignon Blanc!

Vin de Pays de la HAUTE VALLEE DE L'AUDE

If anybody out there is still so blinkered as to believe that the minor regions are still producing nothing but modest wines, I have news for them. The big excitement in this rather lengthily-titled Vin de Pays area is centred on Domaine de l'Aigle near Roquetaillade.You certainly wouldn't normally think of the appellation Vin de Pays de la Haute Vallee de l'Aude as a source of Burgundy-beating Chardonnay but you would be wrong.

Jean-Louis Denois, a young winemaker from Champagne, is making the remarkable Domaine de l'Aigle Chardonnay Classique 1993 (£8.99), a 100% barrel-fermented wine of remarkable quality. The barrel-fermentation gives lovely oak integration (in other words it's not like vanilla essence stirred in at the last moment) and only 15% of the wood is new so as not to dominate the fruit. The result is a very elegant 'white Burgundy' at under a tenner.

Soon the wine will have the Limoux AOC and bureaucracy means that there will be no mention of Chardonnay on the label, so memorise it. M. Denois has recently released the first of his Pinot Noir which weighs in at the same price. It has great colour, more purple than bricky, firm tannins underpinning quite lush fruit and a highly original, non-Burgundian style. Pinot Noir of this quality at this price is a rarity and well worth seeking out. I have a further soft spot for M. Denois in that he uses a quote from me (along with the rather better-known Hugh Johnson and Jancis Robinson, honesty compels me to admit) when advertising in Wine magazine. Clearly a fellow who recognises good writing when he sees it.

Vin de Pays de l'HERAULT

The most interesting wine to come out of this barren but beautiful landscape is the estimable Mas de Daumas Gassac (now with its own Vin de Pays of Haute Vallee de Gassac), a Bordeaux-challenging whopper largely based on Cabernet sauvignon. It all goes back to when Aimé Guibert bought a farmhouse here and toyed with the idea of making wine as a foil to his real work which was in selling fine leathers. He cut a driveway through a bank of soil and one day found one of his guests, an oenologist, peering at the soil profile which it had revealed. A bemused M. Guibert was told that it looked very similar to that at Chateau Latour, the legendary Bordeaux first growth. With the true Frenchman's faith in *terroir*, he set about creating a memorable wine, not just a little something to drink at barbecues. The rest is history. Recent vintages need to spend time in bottle to yield of their all. Mas de Daumas Gassac 1990 (O'B £13.99) and the lighter Mas de Daumas Gassac 1991 (O'B £10.99) are too young for pleasure.

This is designer wine territory, the cutting edge, brave new world and so forth. I've never tasted a mature vintage (rather like hen's teeth) so I'm not sure the wine has the wonderful potential that is claimed for it. Searson's, have the amazingly rare Mas de Daumas Gassac 1979 at a very reasonable £38.00. O'Briens stock a range of vintages from the 1982 at £45.50 .Mas de Daumas Gassac Blanc is terrifically ripe with something of a New World feel to it. A pleasant change from the kind of steroidally-challenged Chardonnays that have become all too common. Figaro (£4.99), a pleasant light red, is made under the direction of the same wine maker. Les Terasses de Guilhem (O'B £5.25) comes from the same estate and can be rather variable in quality but interesting: the red can be big, bouncy and soft with a kind of Chateauneuf quality, the ripe, golden-coloured white seems to have a lot of Viognier in it.

HERMITAGE - see Rhone

JURANCON
Anybody who is becoming bored with the classic varietals should watch out for Jurancon Sec. Jurancon is one of the oldest appellations in France and still only known in this part of the world by manic wine buffs. There are some delicious white wines and no Chardonnay in sight! My current favourite is Jurancon Sec Blanc des Blancs 1992 (SN £6.99), fresh, good weight, dry and flavoursome. It's also *different*, which, to me, is a big selling point. I have a feeling that Jurancon may well become something of a cult with the distinctive taste of the Gros Manseng grape titillating tired palates. Don't confuse Jurancon with the weird, oxidised Vin Jaune of Jura, a region between Burgundy and the Swiss Alps, which vaguely resembles fino sherry but, to me, lacks the zing of Jerez. Cotes de Jura, however, produces rather more conventional red and white wines which I've yet to see in Ireland.

Coteaux du LANGUEDOC
In the ever-changing world of French appellations, Coteaux du Languedoc currently covers a multitude of Mediterranean wines. One of the most attractive and well-priced wines is St Chinian which nobody could accuse of being light but it has a quality that comes quite close to elegance. I'll admit that this is an eccentric view, but I think good St Chinian, with a bit of bottle age, can taste a little like old-fashioned Burgundy. The grapes are the usual Southern mish-mash of Cinsault,

Carignan, Grenache, Mouvedre, and an unpronounceable local variety. The best, in my experience, have a distinctly peppery nose which suggests a good dollop of the classic Syrah. A good example is Saint Chinian Cazal-Viel 1992(QW £5.99), which delivers a lot of ripe, peppery fruit and surprising length for the price. Chateau Milhau-Lacugue 1992 (QW £5.99) is a lot less exciting but the property's second wine, simply called Chateau Milhau 1993 (QW £3.99), dark, soft and quite tannic, offers exceptional value to those, like me, who like gutsy, Mediterranean reds. Don't sip it, have it with a gutsy, garlicky casserole.

Chemin de Bassac Rouge 1993 (MW £6.50) is the first vintage produced by a couple of former teachers, a blend of Syrah, Cabernet and Grenache. It's gianormous with plenty of fruit to support the whopping tannins. Drink it now, having opened it several hours ahead (and double decant it if you have the time); or keep it for two or three years to soften.

Domaine de l'Hortus 1992 (WD£6.59) is dominated by good, earthy Syrah and finishes with a surprisingly herby taste. This is a classic example of why this part of the world is developing such a following: these are new flavours at down-to-earth prices.

Other wines include those formerly known as Faugeres and the unfortunately named La Clape (which gave rise to the old joke concerning 'a nasty case of La Clape'). Try Chateau Pech-Redon 1994 (QW£6.79).

LOIRE

Apart from the chateaux, the Loire is best known as the home of Muscadet. Thankfully it's also the home of some interesting wines like Sancerre, Pouilly Fume, Chinon, Bourgeuil and what have you. But Muscadet, the ubiquitous Muscadet, is the big, big seller.

There are hundreds of muddy-fingered *vignerons* toiling away in the Loire region, applying tender loving care to a grape variety known, ludicrously, as Melon de Bourgogne. From this they produce the famous Muscadet.

Why famous? Can it be because of its enamel-stripping characteristics, so beloved of money-grabbing dentists? Can it be that gastroenterologists the world over see it as a much needed boost to their reflux-oesophagitis business? Or is it, simply, that it's famous because it's famous? After all, I don't think there's a single reasonably sized wine list in the country that doesn't list Muscadet. Muscadet fans - there are quite a few - tell me that it is just perfect with oysters. My problem, perhaps, is that I don't like oysters - raw ones at any rate. Anyway, I always thought Guinness was the thing for sluicing down these ugly bivalves.

Of course, it could be worse. There's Muscadet's first cousin, Gros Plant, which is mercifully little-known in this country. Most examples of this spectacularly unattractive grape have struck me as being a slightly milder and less viscous form of Nitromors. I believe it can be used, with great caution, in the French polishing industry. (After all, being chauvinists we can hardly expect them to use Italian or Spanish battery acid).

My earnest hope for the Muscadet growers is that they root up every single Melon de Bourgogne vine and replace them with Sauvignon Blanc. Or even, God help us, with Grenache Blanc. Then we could drink what they make with a degree of pleasure rather than pain.

It's unlikely, of course. I doubt there's many Muscadet producers who have looked more than a few yards up the road for inspiration.

But if you *must* drink Muscadet, try to know your way around the label. The least repellent tends to be called 'Muscadet de Sevre et Maine sur Lie'; 'Muscadet de Sevre et Maine' will be even less exciting; 'Muscadet', in most cases will be execrable.

The reason why 'sur lie' is important, is because the wine has been aged on the lees, or yeast sediment, giving an extra degree of much needed flavour. Sauvion, probably the best large producer but the least unattractive example I've encountered recently, is called Le Soleil Nantais (SN £6.95) from people called Guilbaud Freres. It has crisp but gentle acidity, lightness with some concentration and a faint whiff of yeast - like freshly baked bread, in fact. Chateau de la Ragotiere (McC£8.50) - current vintage is 1994 - is pleasant enough but I'd prefer to spend the money on something else.

Everyone knows about the two famous Sauvignon-based whites, of course: Sancerre and Pouilly Fumé. Indeed Sancerre and Fleurie tend to be the wine equivalent of steak and black forest gateau for a certain type of *arriviste* diner out -probably because they are easy to remember and pronounce.

Sancerre tends be to be the steelier of the two, Pouilly Fumé being traditionally held to be a bit smoky on the nose. There can be a touch of flint to both but the usual characteristics people look for are a green gooseberry/crushed blackcurrants quality - but rarely in the same turbo-charged form as you will get in some New Zealand Sauvignons. Some can smell a little of cat - which I can't say I like! They should be drunk within two years of the vintage although some of the better wines can kick on a little longer. As they age, they rapidly become rather ordinary though perfectly drinkable white wines.

Baron Patrick de Ladoucette is one of the region's best and most expensive producers, which probably explains his tendency to inspect the vineyards from his helicopter. His flagship Pouilly Fumé Chateau de Nozet Baron de L is a superb wine but rather more expensive than it should be. Expect to pay over £40 for it in a restaurant.

Ladoucette's more modest wines are reasonable value and his Sancerre Comte Lafond can be glorious but, like all Loire Sauvignons, it's got to be very fresh and young. Like its sister wine, Pouilly Fumé Ladoucette, it's really a restaurant wine but, if you find them in a good off-licence expect them to cost around £12 a bottle.

Domaine Vacheron Sancerre 1994 (£12.69) is very widely available and quite fresh and elegant. They also make an uncompromisingly dry rose and an intriguing red Sancerre based on Cabernet Franc. It's not unlike a good Chinon and is best drunk cool. Watch out also for Domaine La Croix Canat (£9.60) and the superb Jean Max Roger 1994 Cuvee CM (SN£10.70). I've also enjoyed the flinty, bone dry Pouilly Fumé Tinel Blondelet 1994 (SN£9.80).

Chateau de Tracy makes a curiously user-friendly wine with a relatively soft edge and very gooseberryish, Sauvignon nose. Mainly in restaurants.

The neighbouring appellations of Menetou-Salon (watch out for the wines of Monsieur Pellé) can produce delicious Sauvignons many of which rival their more famous neighbours. Unfortunately, because they are relatively unknown, they tend be almost the same price as Sancerre and Pouilly Fumé in Ireland. Sainsbury's sell Pelle's Menetou Salon for stg£6.99 - worth putting a case or two in the boot on the way to Holyhead. Sauvignon de Touraine has yet to challenge the more famous names but doubtless times will change.

But the greatest dry white wine of the Loire is none of these. To say that Savennieres is the only wine I've ever tasted that can tackle asparagus is praise indeed but it's also perfectly at home with salmon and crustaceans. Made from the ultra acidic Chenin Blanc grape, the best examples can age and improve for decades because of their high natural acidity. The ultimate comes from Madame Joly whose Clos de la Coulee-de-Serrant 1979 (SN £32.60) is magnificent and only just starting to drink well. It will go on and on. Don't be shocked by the price. This is, quite simply, one of the world's great dry whites and younger vintages, which are drinking well, cost a lot less. Searson's have followed Coulee de Serrant for years and have small stocks of the 1962, 1971, 1976, 1978, 1981 and 1982. There is also a Demi-Sec 1982 (SN £19.55), made specially for Searson's. The delicious Domaine des Baumard 1993 (McC £11.99) is a particularly good buy, very attractive to drink now, not as whoppingly acidic as you might expect a pure Chenin Blanc to be, yet capable of being put away for a decade or more.

The Loire is famous for its immensely long-lived dessert wines made from Chenin Blanc but they do not have anything like the following they deserve in this country. Gaston Huet is one of the greatest producers and if you want to lay some down, talk to Colm Brangan Wines (01 821 6529).

We're not inclined to look to the Loire for red wine, so, if you want to revive the jaded palate, and it's got to be red and light and flavoursome, the Cabernet Franc wines of the central Loire have a lot to offer. The village names are easy enough: Chinon, Bourgeuil and St Nicolas de Bourgeuil.

Chinon, served just cool enough to give a bit of extra tingle is one of my favourite wines to accompany aubergines.

I love the freshness and immediacy of these wines. And they're good value. Bourgeuil Marcel Martin 1992 (QW £5.69) and Chinon Marcel Martin 1992 (QW £6.49) are both from a decent negociant and very attractive quaffing wines.

Andre Barc's unfiltered, single vineyard Clos de la Croix Marie 1989 (SN £8.95), on the other hand, is a stunning wine with outstanding ripeness and concentration which more than justifies the price; it's a great Chinon in a great vintage, drinking now but it will keep a while longer.
LOUPIAC - see Bordeaux
MACON - see Burgundy

MADIRAN
Close enough to Armagnac territory, Madiran used to produce breathtakingly tannic reds based on the local Tannat grape. Now with Tannat joining forces with Cabernet Sauvignon, the picture has changed. Madiran 1990 Plaimont (£6.20) is supple, ripe and has an attractive touch of oak. By comparison to the average claret at the same price this is certainly

more interesting and some of the best wines are not a million miles away from a good Medoc *cru bourgeois*. Findlater's introduced Madiran to Ireland and carry a good range.

MARGAUX - see Bordeaux

MEDOC - see Bordeaux

MINERVOIS

In my student days, Quinnsworth sold a Minervois for £1.49 and it was the sort of stuff you brought to parties only to abandon it in favour of a can of Heineken or, if it was that kind of do, a Pinacolada. It was also the sort of wine that people would bring back from a holiday in France and proudly produce it at Sunday lunch, boasting that it cost less than tap water. Is it any wonder that so many people are inclined to be sceptical about the sweeping changes that have taken place over the past ten years or so? Sure, if you actually go to Minervois itself, or if you concentrate on the cheapest wines in a French hypermarket, you can still get the old rotgut if you really want to. But the Minervois you will get now in Ireland is a very different proposition. This strong shift in quality is no accident. It has been agreed that the deeply unimpressive but big-yielding Carignan grape will account for no more than 60% of the blend by 1999, with Grenache, Syrah and Mourvedre becoming more important. The better producers have already complied - indeed, it was their idea in the first place.

The curiously named Chateau de Gourgazuad 1991 red (DS £4.99) comes from one of the region's top producers. It has lots of ripe fruit, although this was not a marvellous vintage, and the few years it has spent in bottle means that it has softened and yielded up a surprising degree of complexity for such a modest wine. It's quite ready, so don't be tempted to stash away a few bottles for further ageing. The 1993, when it becomes available, promises to be even better and if you're lucky enough to find a bottle of the 1990 you're in for a real treat.

Domaine de Maris Rose 1994 (SV £5.09) comes from a clever and quality-conscious producer; the colour is deep pink or light red, it's dry, fresh, pretty, quaffable. Pink wines are not serious and it's a pity they're not always this affordable. Domaine Maris Carte Noir 1989 (SV £5.99) is a lovely concentrated, chewy red with masses of fruit, a touch of new wood and a very stylish impact. Cuvee Les Meuliers 1993 (£4.99) comes from the leading co-op. It's very modern wine, vinified for good, soft fruit with carbonic maceration giving it a lovely blackberry nose with plenty of backbone. This is one of the easiest-drinking, best-value all-round reds I've had in years.

The very best Vin Doux Naturel Muscat is produced in a northerly corner of Minervois, St Jean de Minervois. Sainsbury's, whom I look forward to welcoming to Northern Ireland pretty soon, do a half bottle for a mere stg£3.99. I import a dozen bottles at a time and scoff it with ripe Roquefort. It beats eating brown Windsor soup while listening to Tannhauser!

MONBAZILLAC
These vaguely Sauternes-like wines have never impressed me.

MUSCADET - see Loire

MUSCAT DE BEAUMES DE VENISE
This is one of the commonest howlers found on wine lists. I must say it conjures up a pretty extraordinary picture. Anyway, Muscat de Beaumes de Venise is the sweet wine that has taken the chattering classes by storm. Why? I suppose it has a lot to do with the fact that its sweet, nice to smell and French. Being French, *ergo* it's sophisticated. The fact that most Beaumes de Venise is rather heavy, cloying and unbalanced is beside the point. Made from aromatic Muscat grapes, the fermentation is stopped by the addition of alcohol which produces a sweet wine which the French, in their odd way, refer to as a *vin doux naturel*. What is *naturel* about this is beyond me although I suppose it may mean that the sugar comes from grapes not from bags. In which case, big deal. Muscat de Beaumes de Venise is not all bad, of course. Jaboulet makes a surprisingly syrupy one but it could be worse. Vidal-Fleury, on the other hand make the best: light, fairly balanced with acidity beneath the sweet-

ness and an enchanting whiff of rose petals on the nose. Muscat de Rivesaltes in general has more complexity, Muscat de Frontignan is heavier and even less attractive as a rule, while some Muscat de Mireval is actually very good indeed - and cheaper.

MUSCAT DE MIREVAL

Let's forget about Muscat de Beaumes de Venise which, despite its grapey, moreish, lusciousness I tend to find dull and boring after much more than a mouthful - Vidal Fleury's version (McC £13.99) is not half bad. Muscat de Mireval Domaine de la Capelle (O'B £12.75) comes from a tiny *appellation* and the leading property. I'm told that the grapes are picked individually - like in the top Sauternais properties. It's surprisingly intense, distinctly Muscat, light in colour and the sweetness is balanced by fresh acidity. It's better than any Muscat de Frontignan that I've yet tasted. Producers in nearby Frontignan don't think Mireval should have a separate appellation. I'm not so sure. Almost as good as Sainsbury's delightful Muscat de St Jean de Minervois (see Minervois), but not quite.

Costieres de NIMES

Costieres de Nimes was formerly known as the Costieres du Gard, though, as Michael Caine would say, not a lot of people know that. Vin de Pays du Gard carries on, however. This is Grenache territory and in many respects it's just like much of the Cotes du Rhone. As in Minervois, they are doing their damnedest to reduce the Carignan content of the wines, because this is the kind of grape that can get you a bad name. Like so many places down here, it used to produce oceans of insipid plonk but now there are quite a few producers doing really exciting things and, naturally, charging more for Costieres de Nimes than they could a few years back. Try Chateau de Rozier 1991 (O'B £7.45) which has a peppery, stewed mulberries whiff, a lovely, soft, fruity impact on the palate and very respectable length. I suspect there's a lot of Syrah in it - it has that very stylish Rhone quality that goes with it.

VIN DE PAYS d'OC:

I suppose everybody knows by now that a revolution has been going on in the South of France and the new buzz phrase is Languedoc-Rousillon. Traditionally this vast sprawling area was content to produce oceans of wine that nobody wanted. In this respect it was quite similar to Irish and other European farming regions where, for some bizarre reason, people are paid to produce foodstuffs that have no market. Just as we have selflessly helped to build the towering beef and butter mountains, so too the Languedoc-Rousillon wine producers valiantly poured hectolitre after hectolitre into the vast depths of the EU wine lake. So well established was this practice that few wine writers ever thought it would change.

The region's biggest customer was the EU who racked their brains and eventually decided to distil all this Carignan and what have you into industrial alcohol - not because it would taste any better (which, no doubt, it did) but because it's easier to find a use for industrial spirit than for undrinkable wine. Mind you, they still managed to sell quite a bit of undrinkable wine to the tourists who flock to the conveniently nearby Riviera and, with some effort, you can still find some of the traditional hooch in the fleshpots of the Cote d'Azur.

Not all Vin de Pays d'Oc wines are exciting. Some are pretty mean and flavourless but they are usually perfectly drinkable. The exciting thing, however, is that a growing number of wine makers are producing well-crafted, down-to-earth, fruit-filled wines which sell at a reasonable price and won't let you down. A few are very good indeed.

They argue about who really got the ball rolling but there's no doubt that Robert Skalli, a Corsican whose family fortune was built on pasta, made a major breakthrough with Fortant de France, a range of classic varietals - Cabernet, Merlot, Syrah, Chardonnay and Sauvignon Blanc - which benefit from distinctly New World winemaking techniques and which sell in Ireland for £4.99. Skalli may have been the first to realise the similarities in climate between the South of France and California. He was certainly the first to put serious money into getting growers to grub up the oceans of Carignan and other woeful grapes which dominated the region and got them to plant grapes that people actually wanted. He also persuaded them to grow grapes in a modern, efficient way and he set up a winery which was amongst the first in France to use what they call modern reductive winemaking techniques.

In simple terms, this means that the wine - from the time the grape is picked to the time the cork is shoved in the bottle is protected from damage, notably oxidation from contact with the air. The result is squeaky clean wines with lots of primary fruit aromas and the kind of ripe fruit you are more likely to find in something from Australia or California. Fortant de France Syrah captures the dark, peppery character of this classic Rhone varietal but delivers so much fruit that you can see how Syrah is actually the Shiraz of Australia. And the fresh Fortant de France Sauvignon Blanc manages to achieve a balance between the green gooseberry varietal character and ripeness of fruit which is very, very rare.

The Skalli gospel soon spread and now there are lots of tip-top producers doing much the same thing, some of them having come all the way from Downunder.

Chardonnay Vin de Pays d'Oc James Herrick, (WD£6.99), a gloriously fresh, zesty wine with lots of varietal character is made by a New Zealander who started his winemaking career in Australia. This is perhaps the most New World white wine from France. Like Hugh Ryman, James Herrick is not content to put his trust in wild yeasts like the Burgundian traditionalists do. So he uses cloned yeasts which will behave predictably. Cloned yeasts often produce a kind of tropical fruits whiff but while this is noticeable on the wine, it still has lots of style and fruit to spare. If you like your Chardonnay big, fresh and fruity, without any oak, this wine offers outstanding value.

The most significant New World winemaker to realise the potential of this part of Europe is BRL Hardy, one of the largest producers in Australia. They own Domaine de la Baume and make the delicious Philippe de Baudin (QW£4.99) wines: big Cabernet Sauvignon 1993 which has plenty of tannin to counterbalance the big, blackcurrant fruit, and a light touch

france

of oak. The Merlot 1992 is softer, even bigger and one helluva mouthful of New World style fruit with a decent dollop of French elegance. The Chardonnay 1994 is in a similar vein to James Herrick's but a little less intense. At £4.99 these wines probably represent the best value in the country at present. A Bordelais blend tete-de-cuvee is, however, the most impressive wine I've yet tasted from this neck of the woods. Sold as Chai Baumiere (QW£6.99), it's superb, elegant, oaky, integrated and enough to scare the daylights out of Bordeaux. I keep going back to it.

BRL Hardy have now been joined in France by another Australian producer, Penfolds, who have teamed up with the French Val d'Orbieu winery to produce a red and a white known as Laperouse (QW£4.99). The white is deeply coloured with generous fruit, just the faintest touch off-dry while the red is soft, slightly peppery, berryish and surprisingly concentrated. It's good to see this Franco-Australian venture eschewing the straight varietal route. These wines are both blends and, if you ask me, all the more interesting for it.

Listel, another major producer, claims to have been years ahead of Robert Skalli and make Domaine Bosquet-Canet Cabernet Sauvignon (SQ£4.79) in the remarkably named Vin de Pays des Sables du Golfe du Lyon appellation. It's packed with jammy Cabernet Sauvignon fruit.

The young English wine maker, Hugh Ryman - whose Australian training shows through in his wines has been producing remarkable good wines at very down-to-earth prices. His critics object to his use of cloned yeasts in white wines, claiming that it makes them all taste the same. But it would be churlish to object to this considering that most of us just want a pleasant white wine with a touch of New World fruit at an affordable price. Not that Ryman's wines are 'me-too' versions of New World wines. His philosophy is that the taste of the actual grape on the vine in the vineyard should come through in the finished wine. To French traditionalists, especially in the Midi, this was something new, eccentric and perhaps not the sort of behaviour that should be encouraged.

Benchmark wines for the southern revolutionaries have to include Ryman's Domaine de Rivoyre Cabernet Sauvignon 1994 (QW £4.99) with its rich, almost baked fruit, fresh blackcurrant quality and just enough spicy vanilla oak to lift the wine into a level of quality which is extraordinary to encounter at a fiver. Likewise Domaine de Rivoyre Chardonnay 1993 (£7.29), a lovely toasty wine with lots of Chardonnay character in the traditional, classical French style. Altogether simpler but with buckets of fresh, fruity, zingy appeal is Ryman's Domaine de la Tuilerie Chardonnay 1994 (QW £4.99).

Domaine du Bosc (McC £4.99) were amongst the pioneers down here and they produce an excellent range of upfront varietals - their dry Muscat and their Chardonnay are simple, straightforward but cleverly executed. They used to be exclusive to Quinnsworth but are now rather hard to find. How come we don't see more of such commercially exciting wines?

Val d'Orbieu is one of the big names in the South of France. Under a variety of labels they sell an exceptionally well made and dependable range of varietals at £5.99 or less - and a delicious, easy drinking Octagon Viognier (SN£6.95), made from the notoriously difficult but delicious white Rhone varietal. Val d'Orbieu's Muscat Sec (£5.99) is wonderfully grapey, dry, aromatic and delicious. Dom Brial Le Pot (MW£5.99) is rather bigger, riper and more concentrated, but still bone dry, a blend of Macabeau and Muscat a Petit Grains.

I first discovered the wines of Domaine Virginie, yet another forward-looking producer of Vins de Pays d'Oc, when I was bowled over by their Viognier 1994 (F/McC/SQ£7.99), a varietal which makes the stunning and expensive Chateau Grillet, one of the rarest white wines around, and Condrieu. Notoriously hard to describe, in its bigger, riper forms Viognier suggests to me a very dry version of Cidona, if you can imagine such a thing. But the Virginie version is light, fruity, lively and enchantingly different from those dull old varietals which throng the off-licence shelves. Virginie's more conventional varieties are all excellent and found mainly on restaurant lists.

La Cuvée Mythique 1993 (SN£7.95) from Val d'Orbieu is not just one
of the most expensive Vin de Pays d'Oc around, it's a glorious blend
of southern grape varieties but with lots of Syrah. With herby, peppery, mulberry fruit and well-integrated oak, I would rather drink this
than many a posh Chateauneuf du Pape and pocket the considerable difference in price. Rapidly becoming a cult wine, La Cuvee
Mythique has a very trendy label and a taste that will appeal to people who like stylish Rhone reds. Drink it now before demand outstrips
supply.

PACHERENC
This is a wine buff's wine, made in the Madiran region, sometimes
with a very distinctive pear-like smell. Try Pacherenc de la Saint
Albert 1991 (F £9.50) for its honeyed fruit and fresh tang. In general,
Pacherenc tastes not unlike Jurancon but with deeper colour. Always
a blend, it depends on rare local varieties for its characteristic style,
although Semillon and Sauvignon sometimes have a walk-on part. Not
exactly thick on the ground which is not surprising considering only 250
acres - the area of a Co Meath grazing farm - is under vine.
PAUILLAC - see Bordeaux
POMEROL - see Bordeaux
POUILLY FUME - see Loire
POUILLY FUISSE - see Burgundy

Cotes de PROVENCE
Most good wine from this region is organically grown - the dry heat
keeps pests and disease at a disadvantage. Keep an eye out for
Commanderie de Peyrasssol in restaurants - a property that puts many
neighbours to shame. Domaines Ott wines are expensive for what they
are - largely due to the fact that the local market is so rich and leisured
the Domaine can charge what they like. The makers very kindly arranged
to have a selection sent to me on the last occasion I mentioned this and I
had the opportunity to taste them all together. I can't say I've been con-
verted. Certainly they are well made but why wouldn't they be? By contrast, Domaine Richeaume Syrah 1990 (S N£10.95) is a wonderful dis-

covery, underlining the fact that good winemaking skills allied to the blessed climate can produce delights. It's huge, dark, jam-packed with really ripe syrah fruit and balanced nicely with softish tannins. It's drinking well now but will happily take a few years in the bottle.

THE RHONE

To most people the Rhone means only one thing - Cotes du Rhone. These three words cover a multitude - from simple, light wines not unlike cheap Beaujolais, to big blockbusters from the likes of Guigal and Vidal-Fleury.

But there's a great deal more to the Rhone than that. There's Chateauneuf du Pape, a wine that can be sublime or perfectly foul. Caution is required here almost as much as in Burgundy. Hermitage is one of the world's greatest wines and is still shamefully (but very attractively) undervalued. And there's a host of other gems just waiting to be discovered.

The Southern Rhone is the home of Cotes du Rhone which, as one of the biggest names in French wine, all too often comes from high-yielding vineyards. This leads to a dilution in flavour and extract, and the *vignerons* screw as much out of the fermentation as possible which leads to light, characterless wines which are notoriously short on taste.

But there's Cote du Rhone and Cotes du Rhone. Guigal, for example, usually produces wine which rivals far more celebrated appellations, although his 1992, made in a poor vintage, comes as a damp squib after the blockbuster 1990. Guigal is one of those fashionable names which you can be sure to find on a certain kind of wine list and certain kinds of South Dublin dining tables. However fashionable the wine may be, it's always amongst the very best in any given vintage. Now, here's a little tip. Vidal-Fleury is part of the same company and now produces wines which are invariably just as good and, occasionally, a little cheaper.

My favourite Cotes du Rhone comes from a much smaller producer than

Guigal. The heavily Syrah-flavoured Domaine Santa Duc 1991 (SN£6.70) from Edmond Gras of Gigondas has masses of flavour, a real peppery nose and a touch of stewed mulberries.

Jaboulet's Cote du Rhone Paralelle 45 is always dependable if a bit more angular than Guigal or Vidal-Fleury and the 1993 is particularly pleasant. It's quite clear that this wine comes from one of the Rhone's most serious producers, even if they are rather large.

If you fancy good Cotes du Rhone but can't stretch to these examples, try a really good Cotes du Ventoux. Jaboulet makes a very dependable, big-boned example (£5.49). Watch out for the Irish-owned Domaine des Anges 1990 (SQ £5.99), a very wholesome mouthful of herby, mulberryish red wine at a really exceptional price which needs wider distribution. Their dearer wines are pretty shockingly tannic but improved winemaking promises to soften the style and make them as accessible as they should be. La Vieille Ferme (£5.99) makes good organic wine with a nice herby, peppery twang.

If, on the other hand, money is no object why not try some of the megawines of the Cotes du Rhone. There's the magnificent Chateau de Fonsalatte Reserve Syrah 1990 (McC £16.69); alternatively you could try Coudoulet de Beaucastel 1990 (McC £10.49), made by the same people who make Chateau de Beaucastel in Chateauneuf. Both wines are gianormous, dark, peppery and pretty tannic but given time they'll be superb. Watch out also for the cheaper but very well made Chateau du Grand Moulas.

Cotes du Rhones Villages, very broadly speaking, is a step-up in quality. Vidal-Fleury's Cairanne is an upmarket Cotes du Rhone. The 1989 (£7.99) is still knocking about and offers mature, complex, serious red wine flavours at a relatively modest price. Other village names to look out for include Rasteau, Visan and Chusclan.

Gigondas used to be part of the Cotes du Rhone Villages appellation. If you taste Gigondas Santa Duc 1991, formerly known as Domaine

Grapillon d'Or (SN£10.60) it's easy to see why it was promoted to its own appellation. There's something reminiscent of fine Graves about this wine - tobacco again! But much more. The startlingly brilliant Les Hauts de Montmerail 1990 (MI £16.95) is the best that money can buy and is in short supply. Even in lesser vintages like 1991 and 1992 this property makes superb wine. Chateau Raspail 1991 (QW £9.19) is relatively, herby and spicy - for robust food.

Can it be the religious connotations, combined with the Irish prediliction for big red wines, that has made Chateauneuf-du-Pape, literally 'the new castle of the Pope', so popular in this country? As a teenager, I recall a pompous young Jesuit expanding the horizons of our education by telling us that Chateauneuf-du-Pape was the most dependable of red wines - which suggested that he had either a rather sheltered upbringing or rather curious taste in wine. The name is a nod to Avignon, where the Papacy spent some time in exile in the fourteenth century, but the wines, as we know them, date back only about 150 years. The phylloxera louse, which devastated most of France's vineyards in the 1870s, didn't much like the stony soil of this part of the Rhone and so Chateauneuf had an advantage over other regions at the end of the nineteenth century.

Chateauneuf du Pape is made mainly from Grenache but the warm climate and the flat stones that cover the vineyards, reflecting heat at night have a major role to play in producing these big, spicy red wines. Cinsault and Syrah are also used, but in small amounts and not by everybody. White Chateauneuf accounts for only one in every sixteen bottles produced and judging by the fact that they are frequently rather flabby, it's easy to see why.

Jaboulet's Chateauneuf du Pape Les Cedres (£10.99) is always good: ripe, plummy, demonstrably well-made. Indeed the current 1992 is even better than usual. Domaine de Vieux Telegraphe 1991 (F £16.95) is very full, luscious and remarkably forward for such a huge wine. Domaine de Vieux Lazaret 1989 (S £12.49) is another sound buy and worth seeking out. Chateau Rayas 1989 (McC £30.00) is, to me, the ultimate

Chateauneuf with its understated label, phenomenal power, extraordinary elegance. Full of contradictions, perhaps, but one of the world's very best reds. Chateau de Beaucastel is not quite in the same league but the 1981 I drank last year was sublime. A delicious 1985 promises well for the future.

Look out also for names like Chapoutier, Vidal-Fleury (a whopping 1990) and Guigal.

The northern Rhone is, in a sense, a rather more serious wine-producing region than the south - not least because of the steep landscape and the dominance of serious grape varieties. It usually produces less wine than all of what comes out of Chateauneuf du Pape alone.

Syrah is the only red grape variety used in the northern Rhone, while Viognier is the white grape behind the rare, fabulously expensive and early-drinking wines of Condrieu and Chateau Grillet. Marsanne and Rousanne go into the other white wines of the region.

Hermitage is the quintessence of Syrah baked in the hot French sun, massively proportioned but with great elegance. The most undervalued red wine in France is undoubtedly Hermitage La Chapelle for which Jaboulet is justly famous. The great vintages are for long ageing, though. I've spotted the blockbuster 1985 for £25 in McCabe's. Try buying Chateau Mouton Rothschild at that price! La Chapelle 1986 (SQ £22.69) is surprisingly ready at this stage and has a wonderfully classic structure with tight French oak locking the whole thing together. It will keep for another decade. White Hermitage is one of the world's great white wines and will age to a kind of honeyed, nutty perfection over twenty or thirty years.

Crozes Hermitage is altogether a lighter, less serious wine but can be delicious in a peppery, spicy kind of way. It accounts for about a half of the northern Rhone's total production. I like Domaine des Entrefaux 1990 (£8.09) and Jaboulet's dearer but more muscular Domaine de Thalabert

1991. Jaboulet's Crozes Hermitage 1992 Les Jalets (£7.69) is soft, generous and very commercial by comparison to the austerely complex Thalabert. Crozes Hermitage Blanc Chevalier de Sterimberg is one of Jaboulet's best white wines and tends to peak around a decade after the vintage.

Cote Rotie (literally, and very appropriately, 'the roasted slope') deserves a lot more attention not least because it is a dry red wine that goes remarkably well with dark, bitter chocolate. Good wine shops should stock fine examples from Guigal and Vidal-Fleury (e.g. La Chatilonne) who seem to make the best. Not much, if any, change out of twenty quid though. One of the reasons why it's so hard to make is the steepness of the slopes. For me the ultimate is Guigal's ultra-rare La Mouline. I had tasted the orgasmically brilliant 1982 recently which has to be one of the finest red wines I've ever tasted with a length that defies both belief and description. Unfortunately it will set you back several hundred pounds a bottle if you can get it. La Mouline, of which only a few hundred cases are ever made, is snapped up by collectors and enthusiasts as soon as it hits the market and is sadly subject to speculators' malign activities.

Be a little wary of Cornas which, in its youth, tends to be as tough as old boots and a real teeth stainer. It's a kind of bucolic Hermitage but given time it opens up and softens to become something scrumptious. Consider putting away Clape's almost opaque, black Cornas 1987 (McC £17.20), from the best producer of all, or Jaboulet's very reasonably priced Cornas 1989 (SQ £12.49) for at least five years.

Other Rhone gems include the Saint Joseph 1989 (SN £12.10), a wine that demonstrates perfectly how Syrah can smell faintly of burnt rubber but not unpleasantly so, from the great Grippat. Jaboulet's Saint Joseph Le Grand Pompée 1994 (£8.59)) is less austere, now mature, but no less enjoyable and really delivers the peppery intensity that characterises good Syrah. The upcoming 1992 is lighter and easier.

Cotes du ROUSSILLON. These are often pretty simple Carignan-based wines. Chateau de Jau 1989/90 (£6.99) is probably the best with lots of soft, fleshy fruit but not as much follow-through as you might expect at the first taste. The 1990 has rather more to it than the 1989.

ST EMILION - see Bordeaux
ST ESTEPHE - see Bordeaux
ST JOSEPH - see Rhone
ST JULIEN - see Bordeaux
SAVENNNIERES - see Loire

Coteaux VAROIS
A few brave properties are showing the way forward in this attractive part of Provence. Take Abbaye Sainte Hilaire (SQ£3.99), for example, made from Cabernet. It doesn't have the *apellation controllee* but haven't we all had some awful bottles that did? It's a humble VDQS with plenty of ripe fruit, no great complexity but a lovely balance. This is real quaffing wine and it has the guts to stand up to robust food. And, at the price, you can afford to quaff it.

Chateau Routas (WD £6.99) is, however, in a much higher quality league. Its Infernet 1992 is an unlikely blend of Grenache, Syrah and Cabernet Sauvignon, aged in small oak, packed with aromatic, berryish fruit; the white Pyramus 1992, although made from the generally uninspiring Rolle, Ugni Blanc and Clairette, is terrifically fresh, full, ripe and generous in flavour. Both wines deliver an awful lot for a modest outlay.
VACQUEYRAS - see Rhone
VOUVRAY - see Loire

GERMANY

Virtually all the German wine sold in Ireland is extremely poor, sometimes downright awful, commercial stuff, the kind of wines that have been so successful in killing off interest in markets right around the world.

After the war, German wine producers had it tough. Cheap imports of French wine were screwing up the domestic market, the economy was in tatters and winemaking equipment was generally very primitive. What saved the industry was the emergence in Britain, Ireland and other non-wine producing countries of a new social class who wanted to drink wine occasionally.

The problem was that they didn't really like the taste of it. And so was born Liebfraumilch, at its best a fresh, quite sweet white wine with an aromatic nose based largely on Muller-Thurgau, which was ideally suited to wean people off lemonade. The most successful brand has always been Blue Nun which, believe it or not, has always maintained quite high standards. However, as the world became rather more sophisticated, Blue Nun has gone into decline although it still exports over a million cases a year, mainly to the US. Billed as the wine you could drink 'right through the meal', it had the same appeal as the Portuguese Mateus Rose. The success of good quality Liebfraumilch spawned a host of woeful imitators and they still dominate the German sector of the Irish wine market. The other undesirable effect of Liebfraumilch's hegemony is that most people think German wine tastes like this. Further confused by the success of the notorious Lutomer Riesling which was never a real Riesling at all, most people think that this great, noble varietal smells of old scent bottles and heaven knows what else.

Great German wine - and there is a lot of it - is made from Riesling. When young the wines are appley, a little floral. With age they develop the classic Riesling aroma of 'petrol' - which is the nearest word we have to describe this extraordinary whiff.

The problem, of course, is finding the good stuff. There is so little interest that it's a brave wine merchant or supermarket chain that stocks even a handful of fine German wines. Enthusiasts might like to know that Mitchell's carry a terrific range as do Searson's; O'Brien's have recently taken on a few goodies while Superquinn and Quinnsworth keep trying to do their best, although in the last year or so they have been seriously discouraged by lack of interest. James Nicholson of Crossgar, Co Down has a fine selection, including the glorious Mosel wines of Dr Loosen. I just wish Irish wine drinkers would give it a try. Good German wines are light in alcohol and gloriously refreshing.

Here are a few guide-lines. Always insist on the word Riesling on the label. Kabinett wines are slightly sweet. Spatleses are a little sweeter but often there's not much difference. When you get to Auslese, the wines are definitely sweet and should be treated as dessert wines. Beerenausleses are wonderful dessert wines and need up to ten years or more ageing before they reach their best. Trockenbeerenausleses are packed with grape sugar, but like all Rieslings they have tongue-tingling acidity to ensure balance. These wines, in a good vintage, will improve for forty years or more and last over a century.

The great Michael Broadbent of Christies is probably the most experienced taster in the world and a great fan of serious German wines. He maintains that they are hard to match with food and I have to say I don't fancy the German tendency to match Ausleses with rich, creamy dishes or game stews. He says that a glass of cool Riesling Kabinett, drunk on a summer evening without any accompaniment apart, possibly, from birdsong in the garden, is the way to do it, and I'm inclined to agree although I've enjoyed the stunning Schloss Vollrads Riesling Kabinet 1989 with bacon and cabbage. The sweeter wines, however, are delicious with simple puddings and with fresh fruit.

Piesporter Treppchen Riesling Kabinett 1993 Rudolf Muller (QW£5.49) is like biting into a green Granny Smith apple - tingling acidity, a slight hon-

eyed sweetness and a wonderfully fresh palate. Some bottles can be
a little sulphury at first but this clears within a few minutes.

Anyone who wants to take up the German challenge has a ready-
made wine course in the form of the Deinhard Heritage (MI £9.95)
range of village wines, beautifully made to express regional character
and stunningly presented in tall, tapering bottles. Deidesheim 1989 is
rich, earthy and very impressive while the Johannisberg 1988 is light,
true riesling with even that hint of petrol, the grape's hallmark when it
has had a bit of age. Neither wine is sweet, nor is it dry. Lovely as a
really stylish aperitif or with mildly spicy food.

Bernkasteler Badstube Riesling Kabinett 1986 (MI £9.20) is fully
mature, light and delicate in the true mosel style, has a hint of sweetness and buckets of fresh, attractive acidity. A perfect partner, incidentally, with Clonakilty back pudding. I love the nineteenth century
label almost as much as the wine when it comes to Hocheimer
Konigin Victoria Berg Riesling Kabinett 1990 (MI£11.70). It's tremendously elegant, light, easy, civilised.

And now some very mature, relatively sweet wines - best drunk with
cheese or something done in a rich, slightly sweet sauce:
Scharzhofberger Riesling Spatlese Vereingte Hospitien 1983 (SN:
£9.85), Eitelsbacher Karthaüserhofberg Kronenberg Riesling Spätlese
1983 (SN £10.70) and Monzinger Frühlingsplätzchen Riesling Auslese
1976 (SN £12.35).

Two world-class wines from German's top estates are available from
Superquinn, both rather drier than you might expect: the full, remarkably
ripe and long Schloss Vollrads Riesling Kabinett 1990 (SQ £12.99) and
the honeyed yet steely, slatey Wehlener Sonnenuhr Riesling Auslese
1988 from the legendary J.J. Prum (SQ £20.79). Not cheap, of course,
but very attractively priced for what they are. Schloss Johannisberger
Riesling Spätlese 1990 (O'B £12.65) is superb: honeyed, crisp, worthy of
a few more years in bottle.

Some of Germany's most interesting wines are from Baden in the south where the generally warmer climate gives higher levels of ripeness. The wines are very distinctive - once tasted never forgotten. By German standards they are positively meaty. Baden Dry (F £5.99) is just that - very dry - but with a really spicy, aromatic nose. Tiefenbacher Stiftsberg Riesling Kabinett 1989 (F £7.50) is light, crisp and not particularly sweet. Munzinger Kapellenberg Gewurztraminer Auslese 1990 (F £10.50) is luscious, spicy with lychees and a gorgeous dessert wine.

Cheap but very sound Germans from Superquinn include: Langenlonsheimer Sonnenborn Ehrensfelser Auslese 1989 (SQ £4.69) and Langenlonsheimer Sonnenborn Scheurebe Spätlese 1992 (SQ £4.69) - not Riesling, not out of the top drawer, but brilliant value. Drink them with blue cheese, or as an aperitif.

ITALY

Italy is second only to Spain as the world's largest wine producer with about 3.5 million acres under vine. The Greeks and the Etruscans brought winemaking to Italy but it has taken a very long time for Italian wine to be taken seriously in the rest of the world. Traditionally, the Italians made very ordinary wine for daily consumption. In places like Tuscany there has been a tradition of fine winemaking for centuries but it is only in the last twenty-five years or so that the outside world has got to see what the real Italian goodies are. For the most part, the vast bulk of Italian wines is cheap and pretty indifferent. Most of what is exported, even Chianti, is not much to write home about. But there is no doubt that there are regions and more particularly producers who are doing very exciting things and, in some cases, producing wine that ranks with the best in the world. In a sense, it is still early days yet for fine Italian wine - certainly as far as we are concerned.

Italy is no less complicated in terms of wine regions than France but we are much less aware of geographical distinctions there. One complicating factor is that there is virtually nowhere in Italy that is without vines. In France and Spain, for example, viticulture is confined to certain well-defined areas.

I am still learning my way around the wines of Italy but I have to say that it's an exciting odyssey and hardly a month goes by but I discover some new gem. Italian wine has come a long way from the days when we were most likely to encounter it in one of those silly straw-wrapped bottles, amusingly known as fiascos, in which bog standard Chianti is wont to dress itself up for the trattoria market.

Here's a quick tour of the regions and a brief guide to what you can get.

Alto Adige: see Trentino

Barolo: These are huge, hard reds for long ageing made way up north in Piedmont from the Nebbiolo grape. I've never had one mature enough to excite me but one name to conjure with is Pio Cesare 1988 (F £18.50). Good Barolo is never cheap but if you like your wines powerful, punchy yet with some complexity, Barolo is for you. The Barolo industry is splitting between modernists and traditionalists but we tend to get the old-fashioned stuff here. I've had one or two superb and amazingly expensive wines from the new wave winemakers but there's no sign of them crossing the water as yet.

Bianco di Custoza: This is usually even less exciting than neighbouring Soave, if such a thing is imaginable. At best, fresh, dry, light, neutral white wines which work with the food of Veneto.

Brunello di Montalcino: This is regarded as being not only Tuscany's most impressive traditional wine but the 'first growth' of Italian wines. It date backs to the 1860s when a winemaker by the name of Biondi-Santi found a turbo-charged clone of Sangiovese which subsequently came to be called Brunello. Biondi-Santi still make Brunello di Montalcino and charge huge prices for it but, by all accounts, the wines aren't what they used to be. On the other hand, Caparzo Brunello di Montalcino 1989(£28) will knock your socks off. You wondered why there was all this fuss about Brunello di Montalcino? This is the reason. Amazing depth and complexity, phenomenal structure and length, a truly great wine and definitely the best Brunello di Montalcino that I've tasted. Rosso di Montalcino is a much lighter wine made for earlier drinking but the best examples are very elegant and attractive medium-weight reds.

Carmignano: Very serious stuff combing Cabernet and the traditional Tuscan Sangiovese to thrilling effect. Villa di Capezzana Riserva 1985 (SN £13.95) is a snip. Their Ghiae della Furba 1981 (£14.50) is like a fully mature Graves.

Chianti: Chianti is made, roughly speaking, between Florence and Siena in Tuscany, largely from Sangiovese. Chianti Classico is a geographical qualification, referring to the heartland of the region. Straight Chianti comes from the peripheries. There used to be quite a lot of Malvasia and Trebbiano, both white grapes, used in Chianti production but now winemakers required to use only 2%. These white grapes now go into Galestro, a simple but pleasantly dry quaffing wine made in the region. Straight Chianti is looked down on these days and even the best of it tends to be simple stuff. One of best cheaper examples is from Rocca della Macie (£5.99) whose Chianti Classico Riserva 1990 (£8.99) is much more serious and complex by comparison. Rocca della Macie is one of those traditional names you can always trust.

Chianti Classico Peppoli 1989 Antinori (SQ £8.99) is a new style: very soft, slight tobaccoish, made by that Tuscan legend, Marchese Piero Antinori. His Villa Antinori Chianti Classico 1990 (£6.99) is always quite rich and very dependable though made in a softer style than most. Chianti Classico 1990 Badia a Coltibuono (SQ £8.99) is more traditional and a really outstanding wine at the price, superb, rich, full, smoky. Castello di Volpaia Riserva 1983 (SN £12.60) is a steal and very claret-like. More recent vintages of Volpaia are also in the highly serious league and well-priced.

Isole e Olena Chianti Classico Riserva 1990 (V £9.99) is a very impressive wine with that tobacco-like whiff that suggests really good Graves. It is one of Tuscany's most respected houses though still a small producer. I would like to see it more frequently. The 'recipe' for Chianti, more or less as we know it today, was drawn up by the Barone Ricasoli about 120 years ago. His descendant, the present Barone makes good, well-priced wine under the Brolio and Ricasoli labels along with a stunning Special Reserve (£18.99)

Chianti Ruffina is not a brand name, it's a sub-region said to make superior wines. Look out for Frescobaldi's elegant Pomino (£12) and the wines of Selvapiana (£10.99).

Frascati: Don't expect anything more than a fresh, light, pretty neutral white wine which is made near Rome. And don't pay more than £5.99. It's made from Malvasia and Trebbiano, so you can't really blame it for lacking breathtaking excitement. Good on a hot day, though, outside a cafe in the town itself. The big brand is Fontana Candida.

Friuli-Venezia-Giulia: There is not much from this area on the Irish market but look out for pleasant varietals from Collavini and Pighin. This is the home of one of the world's best dessert wines, Picolit, a fabulously expensive Vina de Meditazione, as the Italians call it - a wine to be sipped and savoured. Reflecting on its fresh apricot charms can be a delight. Liss Ard House Hotel in Skibbereen is, as far as I know, the only importer. There, it costs £45 for 500 mls.

Gavi: The northern Italians, many of them, are very fashion conscious. As a nation they spend more on clothes than anywhere else in Europe. Gavi is a fashionable white wine and it's now trendy to drink it not only in Milan but also in south Dublin restaurants. I'm not complaining, as I happen to like it and several producers manage to put their wines into bottles which look as if they've been designed by moonlighters from Gucci and Gianfranco Ferre.It's predictably rather dear and is made from the Cortese grape, which is not normally so exciting, in Piedmont. The best examples have good fruit and a fresh, easy character. Gavi 1991 S. Orsola is a good introduction and reasonably priced - around £14 in restaurants. You can try the superior Gavi di Gavi 1992 Villa Lanata (£10.50) and see what a really good one tastes like - and admire the superb packaging that could only be Italian.

Lambrusco: The real thing has a bitter-sweet tang of cherries and a fresh fizziness that's rather attractive. But I've never tasted the real thing -

probably because I don't live in Emilia. You have to go there - and look very hard - if you want the genuine bottle-fermented version. Most Lambrusco is made by cooperatives in a highly interventionist way and the resulting sweetish fizz is lapped up, it appears, by lots of people in the North of England, of all places, and the US. Presumably the Italians have too much sense. Lambrusco, by the way, is also a grape variety but it doesn't seem to have travelled very far. Cabernet has nothing to worry about, it seems.

Lugana: Soave with attitude - if you can find a good one. Made from the rather anonymous Trebbiano grape on the shores of Lake Garda it can sometimes be very dilute and neutral. But the scrumptious Ca' del Frato 1992 (SQ £8.09) is a cracker. I never thought I'd spend over eight quid on Trebbiano which, as one wine writer has said, was given by God as compensation for a dodgy water supply.

Montepulciano d'Abruzzo: No relation of the great Tuscan Vino Nobile di Montepulciano which explains why ill-informed wine enthusiasts whoop for joy as they snap up cases of the stuff, thinking that it should cost ten times as much. Montepulciano is a red grape most of which is grown in Abruzzi. At its best is has gutsy structure, bitter cherry fruit, a good dollop of tannin and reasonable weight. Just the thing with a steaming casserole. Montepulciano d'Abruzzo 1993 Arietta (QW £3.99) is smashing value as just that, as is Miglianico.

Orvieto: This is a beautiful Umbrian town surrounded by vineyards most of which produce some of the most boring white wine in the history of mankind's love affair with the vine. The best on the Irish market is probably Antinori's.

Picolit: See Friuli-Venezia-Giulia

Puglia: The far south of Italy has traditionally had a reputation similar to that of the far south of France - for producing oceans of dreadful plonk which finds its way into industrial alcohol by way of the EU wine lake or into Vermouth blends. Puglia is not a rich place and quality is not usually a big issue. But the Salento peninsula, the heel of Italy's boot, produces some good wines based in part on the local Primitivo grape which may turn out to be the Zinfandel of California. Look out for Salice Salentino Riserva 1990 Candido (£5.95), is a crackingly good, slightly earthy, modestly oaky red wine with oodles of fruit and character. Salice Salentino 1989 Taurino (£8.99) is a touch lighter and perhaps a little more elegant but the Candido is much better value.

Rosso Conero: An up and coming red wine from the Marches, based on the Montepulciano grape of which Rosso Conero Agontano Garafoli (T£9.99) is a fine example: there's lots of red berry fruits, that distinctly Italian high-toned note, a lovely oaky complexity and lots of length. For people who are unfamiliar with serious Italian reds, this wine will be a revelation.

Soave: Soave has been traditionally made with Garganega, but recent changes in the wine law means that Chardonnay, Pinot Blanc and Trebbiano di Soave can now be used to give a bit of character to wines which are all too often rather dull and boring. Soave Classico Superiore 1992 Masi (£6.99) is as stylish as the label and exceptionally well made. The best is probably Soave Classico Superiore 1993 Pieropan (SQ£7.39). Perfect with a plain Parmesan and saffron risotto. I have not yet seen the wines of Anselmi in Ireland but I had some with the local cooking in Verona and was much impressed. Soave, Podere di Caiano is very pleasant, mainly found in restaurants.

Spanna: The same grape as Barolo's Nebbiolo but in this version it's a great deal softer and easier in youth and not vinified for keeping. Try Spanna 1990 (£6.10) - and don't be put off by the revolting label. It's a good rustic red that's been to finishing school. The same grape makes Boca, Gattinara, Lessona, Bramaterra, Fara, Ghemme and Sizzano - but

Ghemme is the only one you're likely to find in Ireland.

'Super Tuscans': These are the wines that fell foul of Italy's notoriously bureaucratic wine laws by using classic varietals like Cabernet and have to go as just Vino da Tavola. Changes are now in train, however, which will create new DOCGs, or proper appellations.Try the stunning, rich, complex, blackcurranty Tignanello 1988 (£16.99) from Antinori which combines Cabernet, Sangiovese and stylish oak ageing, and, if you can afford the price and the time to let it come around, Sassicaia 1987 (SQ £21.50), a pure Cabernet given the full treatment and which rivals Bordeaux's priciest classified growths. Definitely one of the world's greatest red wines. Antinori's Pinot Nero Vigneto Consola 1991 (SQ £14.99) is a remarkable wine: a big, beautifully structured Pinot but not in a Burgundian style at all. From the same stable came the toasty, classy Chardonnay Cervaro della Sala 1988 (SQ £14.99) which is getting rather tired. More recent vintages promise to be superb. Watch out also for wines like Le Pergole Torte, Sangioveto di Coltibuono, Tavernelle (not to be confused with Tavernello!) from Villa Banfi, Coltasalla from Castello di Volpaia, I Sodi di San Niccolo, Sammarco and Solaia. But be prepared to spend very serious money. Searson's have some older vintages of a number of these exceptional wines.

Taurasi: Taurasi is Campania's top region where the big grape is Aglianico. The Aglinaico del Vulture DOC is not far away. Try the fabulous, plummy, tannic Taurasi Mastroberardino Riserva 1982 (SN £10.70) from Campania. Mastroberardino is not only the best producer but the only name you're likely to see much of on the export market.

Torcolato: This is one of Italy's finest and rarest dessert wines which, while made with shrivelled Passito grapes, has a wonderful freshness, liveliness and concentration with a touch of honey and toasted hazelnuts. Very rarely seen but followed by Oddbins who sell occasional lots at about stg£12 per half bottle. A rare curiosity than can be great fun.

Torgiano: A region in Perugia whose reputation has been created by the Lungarotti company using Sangiovese and Canaiolo to produce wines not unlike Chianti Classico. Rubesco 1990 (F £8.99) is rather one dimensional despite brief oak ageing, but older vintages and reservas are fairly impressive. I can't say I like their Chardonnay which strikes me as being rather confected.

Trentino and Alto Adige: An increasingly good source of reasonably priced fresh wines - mainly white - for example the Pinot Grigio Atesino Alto Adige1994 (QW £3.99) which is dry, clean, fresh, easy and affordable. Trentino Moscato Giallo 1993 Mezza Corono (MI £6.90) is packed with sweetish Muscat fruit and immediate gratification. A lovely accompaniment to salty pork rillettes, for example. A further example from the excellent Mezza Corona range is the plummy, baked-fruit, dark red Trentino Teroldego Rotaliano 1992 (MI£6.90) made from a local grape variety. Trentino Pinot Grigio Mezza Corona 1993 (MI £6.50) is a really elegant, dry white. The distinctive orange label of Rotari Brut Trentino (MI £12.65) looks uncannily like that of Veuve Clicquot - and the quality of this Northern Italian sparkling wine is not too far off good Champagne. This gives plenty of style for a very fair price. The varietal thing is in full swing in this Northern, cooler part of Italy and there are some crisp, slightly stalky Cabernets and Merlots to be had. Watch out for elegant wines from La Vis (T£6.99), including a yummy Pinot Nero, a light, delicate Chardonnay and a particularly attractive Pinot Grigio. Watch out for first-rate wines from Alois-Lageder, especially on good restaurant lists.

Valpolicella and Bardolino: These are the definitive red party wines, cheap and cheerful, made in the Veneto region up North, from Corvina, Molinara and Rondinella. Valpolicella Classico is the original Valpolicella area and accounts for less than half of the total production. Valpolicella Superiore simply means that the wine has a minimum alcohol content of 12%. However, most Superiore is made by the ripasso method which involves using grape skins from the production of Amarone. This boosts the alcohol and the extract and you end up with something which is frankly more interesting than your basic Valpolicella. Masi Campo Fiorin (£8.99) is a lovely example with a distinctive taste of bitter cherries. The most widely available quality Valpolicella is also from Masi (£5.99). Bolla is good commercial name, though I have to say that straight Valpolicella is nothing more than a simple, light, fairly crisp red wine. Recioto della Valpolicella Amarone (£14-£18), made from partially dried red grapes, achieves alcohol levels in the region of 15% and contain some residual sugar. They are whoppers and elegance is not their strong point but Masi's are worth looking at. The top Amarone comes from Quintarelli (over £20).

Vernaccia di San Gimignano: These can be neutral to the point of virtual oblivion but some examples are definitely better than the standard Tuscan whites based on Trebbiano. The local grape hereabouts is Vernaccia which oenologists believe is not related to the vague, catch-all label of 'Vernaccia' used elsewhere. The best wines indisputably come from Terruzi & Puthod whose 1992 Terre di Tuffi (SN £13.25) is an interesting 'designer' wine in a relatively neutral style but with a faint touch of oak.

Vino Nobile di Montepulciano: Although made largely with straight Sangiovese and not the super-clone version Brunello, at its best it can rival Brunello di Montalcino. But even modest efforts are pleasant - try the Vino Nobile di Montepulciano 1992 Cecchi (QW £5.99) with its elegant nose tinged with licquorice and fairly high, racy acidity. Lovely dark red, very Italian. Rosso di Montepulciano is a lighter wine, made for earlier drinking.

NEW ZEALAND

There's no love lost between the Australians and the New Zealanders. A recent poster campaign for a Kiwi lager had the following copy line: What do you call a sophisticated Australian? A New Zealander.

Although we think they speak the same, they don't. Kiwis seem to have turbo-charged Australian accents and a tendency to refer to 'fush and chups'. They also go to bed earlier, drink marginally less and occupy a very beautiful, rather green country. The green is the clue to New Zealand wine. Cool microclimates mean that certain parts of New Zealand imitate the marginal character of Burgundy. The big success story, of course, has been Sauvignon Blanc. Good New Zealand Sauvignons smell pungently of green gooseberries, blackcurrant leaves, asparagus, green pepper. Some of them are grassy too. These wines are aggressively varietal and some people prefer the more muted tones of Sauvignon as expressed in a Sancerre, for example. Cloudy Bay was the first New Zealand Sauvignon to grab the imagination in Ireland. It's a cult wine, a very good Sauvignon indeed but not significantly better than many rivals, notably Hunter's. Like certain other New Zealand wines, it's in short supply and has to be rationed. Hence the panic to buy it as soon as it's released. I suspect many Cloudy Bay drinkers are attracted by the label rather than what's inside the bottle - which demeans a very good wine.

The New Zealand wine industry was founded by immigrants, mainly from Eastern Europe, who were fond of concocting hideous, brown, sticky for-tified wines from obscure grape varieties. When not drinking that they were given to making a kind of downunder Liebfraumilch for local consumption - hence the vast planting of aromatic but distinctly naff Muller-Thurgau grapes. But times have changed and the new New Zealand wines are world class.

They are certainly different from Australians. The distance between Marlborough and the nearest Australian vineyards is roughly the same as that between Dublin and Moscow. The difference in styles is similar.

While Australians do battle with the heat and, against the odds, struggle to prevent over-ripeness and the loss of fruit flavours, the New Zealand climate is quite cool. Hence the bright-as-a-button tastes which jump out of the whites and the sometimes rather green, leafy, even stalky reds. There can be a certain sameness about New Zealand Sauvignon. Once you've tasted the wild, green, grassy. stalky, sherbety style of one you've pretty well tasted them all. But I like them, even if some wines are almost brutally varietal. If this is not your style, the Chardonnays are much milder but still very fruit-driven. I suspect we'll soon be welcoming some impressive, though expensive, Pinot Noirs to these shores before long.

We drink very little New Zealand wine and yet there seems to be quite a lot of it about. I suspect that this means it has become fashionable and while it graces the salons of Dublin 4 and the smart restaurants it is not yet posing any great threat to Piat d'Or.

Aotea makes a good Sauvignon Blanc 1993 (£8.99) although it's not in the first division.

Babich are not sufficiently well-known and I wish we had some of their explosively fruity Sauvignons here. However the Chardonnay 1992 Hawkes Bay (MI £9.95) is not half bad and the Cabernet Sauvignon (MI £9.95) is rich despite a leafy, stalky nose which, unlike Robert Parker, I happen to like a lot.

Cloudy Bay was New Zealand's first designer wine. When it arrived first in Ireland there were Jaguars and BMWs cruising the off-licences of

South County Dublin for it. The name was made, justly, by the crisp, gooseberries-asparagus-green peppers-blackcurrant leaves-sherbet Sauvignon Blanc (£13.95) but the Chardonnay (£13.95) is more subtle and complex in an unexpectedly generous, buttery style. Demand for Cloudy Bay Sauvignon Blanc significantly outstrips supply and it's very hard to get. This is crazy. It's a good wine but I suspect that most people drink it because of what it says on the label and not because of what's in the bottle. Several New Zealand wines match it in quality, notably Hunter's, albeit in a different, rather more restrained style - though Cloudy Bay seems to be the pick of the crop in the difficult 1995 vintage. There's also a very expensive but delicious Cabernet Merlot (SQ £16.99) with that leafy, stalky quality that I persist in liking whatever Robert Parker may say. Cloudy Bay's Pelorus 1989 (F £17.00) is a high tech sparkler and in very short supply. I feel it's going to get a lot better. At the moment it's not a major threat to Champagne but very full, fruity and fresh all the same.

Cooks are unusual in being a very big winery - New Zealand is the land of small producers - and they make buckets of very palatable, simple, easy-to-drink wines. The Cabernet Sauvignon/Pinot Noir 1993 (£5.29) is a weird and rather wonderful combination which makes Beaujolais look rather dull. Cooks' upmarket Stoneleigh Sauvignon Blanc 1993/4 (McC £9.09) is a decent, sherbety, fresh wine with lots of varietal character - and very, very dry.

Hunter's, in my view, make the best Sauvignon and Chardonnay at the price. Jane Hunter's brilliantly assertive Sauvignon Blanc 1994/5 has plenty of that wild, green, pungency to it but with a very impressive almost Loire-like austerity underpinning all the razzamataz (£9.49). It's one of my favourite New Zealand wines. The Chardonnay 1991 (£9.49) is a complex, nutty, buttery affair that makes many Oz equivalents seem rather crude.

Matua are amongst New Zealand's most elegant wines. Even the Sauvignon Blanc 1994 (£9.99), which you expect to be savagely green and pungent is quite gentle and almost Loire in style, suggesting a leafy Pouilly Fume while the delicious, under-stated Chardonnay 1993 (£9.99) owes a great deal to cool growing conditions. Well worth a detour.

Montana produces wonderful wines despite its vast size. The Sauvignon Blanc (£6.99) is one of the best and one of the cheapest. It has all the character you want: freshness, a strong nose of crushed blackcurrant leaves, plenty of fruit, acidity and zing. Brilliant. The Chardonnay (£6.99) is a lovely, simple, gentle wine and the Cabernet Sauvignon (£6.99 is remarkably ripe, plummy and not at all green, leafy and stalky. The excellent Lindauer, a classic Champagne blend of pinot and Chardonnay (£11.99) is one of the New World's most subtle and attractive sparkling wines.

Morton Estate is not as well known as the wines merit. I'd single out their Sauvignon Blanc Hawkes Bay 1993 (DS £6.99) as a peer of Montana's any day - very similar in style but perhaps with a little more richness underneath the typical New Zealand green, grassy, sherbety pzazz. The Chardonnay, in typical New Zealand style, has a ripe, buttery style with a scintillating backbone of acidity and a faint whiff of oak. The Cabernet/Merlot (McC £8.95) is attractively jammy, rich and heartwarming but has sacrificed the traditional and much derided Kiwi stalkiness for something rather loose-knit and amorphous. But great value, like Montana.

Nobilo's make wines with so much flavour they can be almost overwhelming. The Sauvignon Blanc (SQ £7.09) is amazingly full of stewed gooseberry fruit, zesty acidity and a lovely, deep colour - at a remarkably good price. Some would say that it's trying too hard to borrow a kind of Australian opulence but it's a helluva of a wine whatever way you look at it. Poverty Bay Chardonnay (SQ £6.99), as served on British Airways, is a real bargain. and the slight corky problem that dogged this wine a few years ago has been long solved.

Selaks may sound as if it's made from senna pods but it's the name on a very attractive Sauvignon Blanc Marlborough 1993(McC £7.25) in something akin to the Montana style. There is also a good light Chardonnay.

Villa Maria are very sound, fresh, straightforward wines delivering typical New Zealand zestiness at a reasonable price.

Wairau Valley wines are amongst the best value New Zealanders around though they are not widely available. Like Matua, they eschew the wilder, greener, racier characteristics which are shared by most of their compatriots and offer a good bridging point between classic French whites and the opulence of conventional New World styles. The agents are Terroirs of Donnybrook.

Wines which I hope we will see arriving sometime in 1996 must include the stunning Jackson's Estate Sauvignon Blanc and the exciting Te Mata Coleraine range.

NORTH AMERICA

It's easy to see why California is called the Wine State. Although there are serious wineries in other States, notably Oregon and Washington, California accounts for by far the most wine produced in the US. Wine was first made here by Franciscan missionaries in the late 17th century and there were scattered outbreaks of table wine production, almost all by Italian or German immigrants, until America went completely mad and introduced prohibition. At this point, Californian vineyard owners made a fortune growing grapes to produce juice for home winemaking, a pastime that was both legal and lucrative. The mind boggles as to what kind of hooch New Yorkers brewed up in the basement from California grape juice concentrate but it was probably safer than the illegal hard stuff which was based on potatoes and heaven knows what else.

In the 1960s a New Yorker magazine cartoonist hit two nails on the head with the caption 'I'm afraid it's just a naive domestic Burgundy but I think you'll be amused by its presumption': the sheer ghastliness of the pretentious wine buff and the embarrassment with which Americans greeted the first generation of Californian wines as we know them.

Now, the US is a nation of wine drinkers - at least as far as the aspiring classes are concerned. Jug wines abound but the small, quality conscious and almost always expensive 'boutique' wineries have cult followings and winemakers can become superstars - like Bob Mondavi.

In Ireland there are three levels of Californian wine. First of all there's the very commercial stuff which is aimed at new recruits to wine drinking. Then there's the £8-£9 a bottle which is good, commercial wine, as a rule, but it faces stiff competition from Europe and Australia. Then there's the sky's-the-limit wines which are understandably very thin on the ground but many of them can hold their heads up with the finest in the world. Here's a quick guide to what's available in Ireland - and a few others which I hope will make it soon to the Ould Sod, whoever that may be! Incidentally, the best range of North American wines in Ireland is, oddly, not in a shop, but a restaurant. The Park Hotel, Kenmare, has a superb list, including names like Martha's Vineyard, Randal Grahm, Au Bon Climat and the ironically-titled Far Niente ('for nothing'). I drank the Dunn's Vineyard 1987 Cabernet Sauvignon there and came close to swooning. This is first rate wine, very expensive, of course, but the sort of thing that puts you in mind of claret in a glorious vintage from a first growth. I'm serious.

Accacia: Just taken on by Searson's, this new arrival have made a name for themselves with surprisingly Burgundian Chardonnay and Pinot in Carneros.

Allen Estate: Delicious cedar-wood scented Cabernet Sauvignon (MI£14) from Jim Allen, a rare creature: a sane Californian.

Beaulieu Vineyards: One of the great names in California - and one that has been around for a very long time, Beaulieu Vineyards which I insist on pronouncing 'bewley' much to the Americans' bemusement, is mainly found in restaurants. The lovely Beautour Cabernet Sauvignon 1989 (McC £9.99) is supple, fleshy, spicy, delicious. George de Latour Private Reserve Cabernet Sauvignon is rich, expensive and age-worthy - but not in the same league as the equivalent wine from Beringer.

Beringer: I find the basic Berginger range a bit dilute and ordinary, while their Cabernet Sauvignon Private Reserve 1986/89 (V/R/G/T £29.50) is undoubtedly one of the world's great red wines - as it should be, of course, with that price tag. It has a taste and a complexity and a power and a subtlety that almost defies belief and puts me in mind of Chateau Latour. Beringer Private Reserve Chardonnay 1992 (T £19.99) is as good as many considerably dearer wines: complex, nutty, long but not over-ripe.

94

Blossom Hill: Highly commercial, cleverly packaged wines to woo consumers - mainly young and female, apparently - off fizzy drinks, and very successful within these bounds.

Bonny Doon: This is the winery run by the eccentric Randal Graham, known as the Rhone Ranger because of his love of Rhone varietals like Syrah, Grenache and Viognier. His brilliant dessert wine Muscat Canelli Vin Glaciere has been banned by the EU - for being too natural! La Cigare Volant (JN stg £10.99) is a glorious Chateauneuf-style red with a curious whiff of spice and fennel on the nose. He makes the modestly-titled Bloody Good Red and Bloody Good White for the UK chain Oddbins where you can have them for a mere stg £6.99. Crying out for an Irish agent but prices are a little high for the mainstream.

Buena Vista: Marginally more exciting than Christian Brothers - the wines, that is.

Christian Brothers: Not Christian Brothers as we know them but some form of de la Salle order make these rather ordinary wines. I find the Cabernet particularly lean and charmless.

Clos du Bois: They make good wines - particularly their rich, ripe, attractively smoky Merlot 1989 (McC £9.99). The equivalent Chardonnay can be a little flabby.

Clos du Val: The wines are made by the Bordeaux-trained Bernard Portet and are supposedly famed as elegant, silky reds. I can taste the fact that they are seriously made but to me they completely lack fruit, charm and value-for-money. An unfashionable viewpoint, but there it is.

Columbia: A winery in Washington State founded by Englishman David Lake in 1962. Columbia's wines were discovered not so long ago by Superquinn who have followed them loyally ever since. Columbia

Cabernet Sauvignon 1986 (SQ £8.09) I tend to be find rather hard and light on fruit and the Chardonnay is not particularly wonderful but the superb Columbia Pinot Noir 1989 (SQ £8.99) is remarkably Burgundian even down to the light colour belying a great depth of distinctive pinot flavour.

Concannon: An old winery in Livermore Valley with Irish origins. The unusual Petite-Syrah (MI£10) is dark, lush and peppery, while the Sauvignon Blanc (MI£9.50) is crisp, dry and nicely varietal.

Domaine Drouhin: Some Oregon Pinot Noirs have been so success-ful that Robert Drouhin, one of Burgundy's best-known names, has set up a winery there. The Domaine Drouhin Pinot Noir 1990 (T £25) is worthy of the hefty price tag though it needs either a few years ageing or several hours in the decanter. Actually, it's better than some similarly-priced wines that Drouhin is making back home in France. Although an expensive wine, this is the equivalent of very serious Burgundy and a very successful early vintage by a new winery. Delicious.

Fetzer: A successful Mendocino winery making attractive up-front wines including the modest Bel Arbres blend. The dark and plummy faintly vanilla-ish Fetzer Zinfandel 1990 (£8.09) is an exciting wine, a value-for-money example of what this native American grape can do. Fetzer Sundial Chardonnay 1990 (£8.09) is good, simple, modern California Chardonnay that does not hit you over the head with a malletful of ripe fruit.

Firestone: Rarely seen range of rather heavy, alcoholic varietals from Santa Ynez Valley.

Gallo: This range of cheap varietals once became so much part of Quinnsworth that it was quite a shock to see these familiar wines ulti-mately go their own way but they have become more widely available. As always, it is amazing that the biggest winery in the world can produce such consistent wines at remarkably cheap prices.

The straight Gallo range (£4.49-£4.99) are unapologetically commercial with some displaying surprisingly high levels of residual sugar. As such, they are good recruitment wines. On the other hand, Gallo Sonoma Cabernet Sauvignon (£9.99) and Gallo Sonoma Chardonnay (£9.99) are very serious wines indeed showing ripe fruit balanced with a rather classical structure of acidity, oak and tannins. There is also a *tete-de-cuvee* Chardonnay to rival many fine white Burgundies and a similar but even dearer Cabernet with immense character and great ageing potential.

Glen Ellen: Despite the cloying radio commercials I have to say that the wines are very decent and have recently been enjoying a lot of interest. Glen Ellen Proprietor's Reserve Cabernet (£4.99) is outstanding at the price, followed closely by the very charming but less complex Merlot. Glen Ellen Proprietor's Reserve Chardonnay (£5.79 is mildly oaked and very attractively priced.

Heitz: Not yet available on the Irish market but one of the great Californian names, Heitz's best-known wine is the Martha's Vineyard Cabernet Sauvignon which is made in a very traditional style and needs time to emerge as a big, ripe, luscious but immaculately structured red worthy of Bordeaux in a great vintage. The Chardonnay can be closed when young but opens up to a glorious buttery but dry complexity at about six or seven years. Expensive stuff.

Iron Horse: Located in the Russian River Valley, Iron Horse makes decidedly claret-like Cabernet Sauvignon with classic, French structure. Easy enough to drink young, it comes into its own around about five to eight years old. Expensive and not yet on the Irish market. Their second label, incidentally, is called Tin Pony.

Paul Masson: Not the worst of the ultra-commercial producers but, beyond that, there's not much left to say.

The wines of Robert Mondavi are perhaps the most famous of the Californians and his reserve wines are stunning. I was once served his Cabernet Sauvignon Reserve 1983 against Chateau Margate 1983 in a blind tasting. While I managed to distinguish between them it took quite a lot of sniffing and slurping which just goes to show that this is a wine to conjure with. Mondavi's Reserve Chardonnay is burgundian and buttery, very classic. The idea, it appears, is to try to copy great French classics. There should be no shame in that considering how successful they are. The more ordinary Mondavi wines are reasonably impressive but dearer than they should be. Mondavi Cabernet Sauvignon 1988 (£13.99) and the jammy, unbalanced Pinot Noir are prime examples while the Mondavi Woodbridge (£8.99) wines remain unexceptional and appear to be trading on the Mondavi name.

Domaine Mumm, owned by the Champagne of the same name, makes the best American sparkling wine I've ever tasted. Mumm Cuvee Napa (£11.99) must have struck fear into the hearts of the Mumm management when they first tasted it.

Murrieta's Well: Sergio Traverso's unbelievable Zinfandel 1991 (T£16) comes from the Livermore Valley and contains a whopping 16% alcohol. However, this potential monster of a wine is really a gentle giant. It has terrific colour - almost black. There is plenty of American oak, as a result of two years in new casks. There are mountains of fruit - bramble jelly sort of thing and relatively soft tannins. The length goes on and on and on. But the extraordinary thing is that this wine does not actually ram pepper up your nose and taste like something that has spent too long in the sun. There's also a blockbuster Cabernet and Merlot combination with the addition of 14% Zinfandel which is sold as Murrieta's Well Vendimia Red (T£18.99). Production is quite small - the whole property only makes 5,000 cases a year which makes a typical classed growth in Bordeaux seem almost gigantic by comparison.

Niebaum: Terroirs in Donnybrook stocks a number of very serious Californians including the remarkable Francis Coppola Family Cabernet Franc 1990 (T £12.90), the celebrated Niebaum-Coppola Rubicon 1982 (T £28.00),

Quady: Essencia Orange Muscat (JN stg £6.99) and Elysium Black Muscat (JN stg £6.99) are amongst the most alluring half bottles of dessert wine you will ever encounter. Essencia has a tang of marmalade while the intriguing dark red, fresh, grapey, aromatic Elysium is quite weird and wonderful - the grapiest wine I've ever tasted.

Ridge: Widely recognised as being amongst California's top producers of Zinfandel, their wines have reached cult status and can be got from James Nicholson of Crossgar, Co Down from around stg £14.99. I find them rather heavy and over-alcoholic but maybe I've tried them too young (the wines, not me).

Sebastiani: A recently introduced range of moderately commercial varietals from Sonoma.

Stag's Leap: Definitely one of the tip-top producers in California, this Napa winery was founded by a Classics professor. The very rare Stag's Leap Cask 25 (T £48.00) ranks with some of Bordeaux's best - and so it should. Stag's Leap has a way with Cabernet, but their Chardonnay, too, is made in a very classical French style with a little touch of New World oomph which makes it sing. Not easy to find even if you can afford it.

Sutter Home: Particularly lack-lustre range of budget varietals. Just not worth it.

Wente: One of the oldest wineries in California, Wente have been innovative winemakers in the Livermore Valley. Their wines are successful mid-market varietals rather in the same mould as Beringer but with a touch more excitement in the whites.

PORTUGAL

I discovered Portuguese wines as an impecunious student teacher and I have ever since blessed the name of Superquinn for providing me with a decent everyday red wine at an affordable price. That was about twelve years ago and the wine was Serradayres - which I pronounce serra - die -rays, but the Portuguese manage to make it sound like someone with a very heavy cold clearing their throat. (If you're worried that your Portuguese winespeak lacks street cred, just leave out all the vowels and remember that vinho verde rhymes with weird).

Anyway, its hard to evoke the spirit of the early eighties, those strange days before the arrival of Australian wines and, indeed, before even the Bulgarians made a name for themselves with affordable plonk that you could bring to a dinner party and certainly well before Muscat de Beaumes de Venise wrapped its sticky fingers around the minds of the Dublin 4 set. It was a time ripe for big, earthy, unapologetic red wines with a modest price tag and that's just what Portugal does very well. The earthiness is very distinctive and difficult to define - but once you encounter it you will know it forever more. Much of it comes across on the nose and, to use a very crude and inadequate image, it suggests, to me the same kind of rubbery whiff that I associate with the Spanish sparkling Cava wines. But I like it.

There are, of course, some very modern Portuguese wines which, with careful cloning of vines, use of imported grape varieties and squeaky-clean 'reductive' winemaking, to use the buzz word, manage to taste positively international. The value-for-money JP wine from Peter Bright at Joao Pires are prime examples and the value-for-money Leziria has only the faintest hint of the old Portuguese whiff.

And now a quick word about why we don't look to Portugal for white wines. Unlike places like Australia and Chile, the average Portuguese winemaker does not lose any sleep agonising over what kind of wines we - that is the residents of these islands - want to drink. Instead, they occasionally wonder why the hell we don't like wines like those beloved of the Portuguese. Nowhere is this more evident than in traditional white wines. Traditionally - and it still applies in many places, if you gave a Portuguese consumer a glass of fresh, well-made, carefully-fermented white wine you would be told that this was foreign muck. Bizarre as it may seem, the traditional Portuguese taste has been for flat, oxidised, singularly dead white wines - precisely the sort that we can't stand. Many wineries, however, are making nice fresh, clean, simple whites for the export market (Grao Vasco's white Dao springs to mind) which is very good at the price, while giving the old boys at home a taste of their true heritage in the form of mawkish, oxidised battery acid. I mention this just in case you stray beyond the Algarve and wander into a corner bar for a quick snifter. Stick to the red, just in case.

It's odd to think that the Portuguese helped to start the Irish wine revolution which is now reaching fruition. In the 1960's many a sophisticated young couple around town would wash down their prawn cocktail and well-done steak with a glass or two of Mateus Rose before going on to do the Hucklebuck at the Television Club. (I have this on good authority, having been tucked up in bed myself at the time). Mateus Rose made its maker, Sogrape, very rich and they now make a wide range of very sound, dependable and modern wines which are worth seeking out. Searson's carry some of them. Don't let the Mateus Rose connection put you off.

Portugal still suffers from the fact that it has spent centuries in isolation from the rest of the wine world, even from Spain. Although they were amongst the first countries to introduce wine laws, the wine industry is only now starting to embrace high tech approaches which are commonplace elsewhere. The Portuguese are rightly proud of their native grape varieties like Touriga Nacional, the basis of Douro and Dao wines, and the unusual Periquita but international classics like Cabernet Sauvignon and Merlot have made little headway.

Alentejo: Watch out for the wines from the cooperatives of Reguengos de Monsaraz and Borba. These establishments are exceptions to the general rule that Portuguese co-ops make wines exclusively for the eccentric local taste and are also disproving the traditional saying that Alentejo is 'the land of bread and bad wine'. Adega Coop de Borba Reserva 1988 (£5.99) is dark, soft, easy and surprisingly long at the price. Esporao Reserva 1989 (SQ £8.99) comes from a huge, modern estate with a cellar so deep that they have candles burning just to make sure that there's enough oxygen. It's a very complex, elegant, stylish, oaky red wine, definitely one of Portugal's best, but bear in mind that you can pick it up for stg £4.99 in Oddbins in the UK. It's so good it deserves the widest possible audience. The highly traditional Quinta do Carmo 1987 (SQ £15.39) has received investment from the Rothschilds of Chateau Lafite and should produce interesting results in due course.

Bairrada: This was a thriving northern wine region two centuries ago but the industry was wiped out when regulations were introduced to protect the nearby Port business. It is still recovering and only gained Regiao Demercada status in 1979. Virtually all of the wine is red, made from the local Baga grape. Most of the wine made by smallholders is incredibly tannic, but the most widely available Bairrada comes from Alianca (otherwise known as Angelus) (£4.39) who de-stem the grapes to minimise this problem. Sogrape's Bairrada wines (SN£5.99) are light, fresh and elegant.

Colares: Traditionally regarded as one of Portugal's most distinguished wines, Colares is grown in sand dunes not far from Lisbon and gets vinified, stalks and all in big concrete tanks. Nicely scented, it is literally unbearably tannic much before twenty years in the bottle. A curiosity, of course, but not really worth the effort and the hefty price tag. Carvalho, Ribeira & Ferreira are experimenting, however, and perhaps they will manage to produce a Colares for the modern palate.

Dao: It's still suffering from a major re-structuring of the industry which took places three decades ago. It meant that co-operatives came to dominate the region and although this has now changed some of the bad habits persist - like keeping the skins in contact with the wine for too long and late bottling. Too much red Dao is tough, tannic and charmless. The whites are almost all execrable but there are some fresh ones starting to appear. Several good value wines come from Caves Sao Joao (£3.99 - £4.99) but be prepared for old-fashioned woody tastes and buckets of tannin. Great value, though, if you like your red wine rough and ready. Fonseca's Terras Altas (£6), both red and white, is dearer but a lot more refined. Grao Vasco (SN£6) red is similar but the white is outstandingly fresh and fruity. Red Dao, incidentally, is quite viscous.

Douro: We're talking here about the great river before it reaches port territory. Consider the big, bouncy, very serious Douro Reserva 1987 (SQ £7.25). If you're looking for Portugal's top red wine, try Barca Velha 1983 (SQ£28) which is fabulously concentrated, oaky, minty, long and luscious, also in selected Sainsburys £18 in the UK.

Ribtejo: Leziria (SV/R £3.99) is still winning applause - including a gold medal at the Wine International awards. The red is a gulpable blend of Pinot Noir and Periquita and offers terrific value for money. The white is an attractively grapey, Muscat-influenced wine which will offend nobody - but in the same league. The negociant company of Carvalho, Ribeira & Ferreira are known for their cheap, cheerful and vaguely old-fashioned Serradayres 1993 (SQ £4.29) from Ribatejo but don't be tempted by the white. The same company produce quite a complex, fully mature Garrafeira 1985, also based on Ribatejo wines (SQ £6.99).

Setubal Peninsula: One of Portugal's most progressive wineries is Joao Pires where Peter Bright, an Australian winemaker, has been at work for over a decade. Watch out for their remarkably cheap JP wines (£3.99). The white is mainly muscat-based, ripe, grapey, aromatic. The red is light and juicy, low in tannin, very gulpable and can be served cool. Joao Pires are good with Muscat. Try the faintly off-dry Joao Pires Branco (SQ£6.99), a brand now owned by the US company Heublein, or really push the boat out with their stunning Moscatel de Setubal (£13.09 but hard to find), a fortified dessert wine which smells pungently of grapefruit marmalade. When Sainsbury's open in Northern Ireland we will be able to get hold of Joao Pires' Quinta da Bacalhoa, a big, soft, Cabernet-based red for a mere stg £4.99.

J.M. da Fonseca, who have been with Mitchell's for yonks, make stunning Moscatel de Setubal (MI£10) too, including a superb 20-Year-Old (MI£16) which puts me in mind of very good and unusually fruity tawny port. There is an attractive and modern dry white, Albis (MI£6) which deserves to be better known. But they also produce some of Portugal's most compelling reds - in particular the Cabernet-based Quinta da Camarate 1987 (MI/McC£8) which is soft, easy, fully-evolved, lightly oaked and remarkable value. Their 100% Periquita 1992 (MI/SQ£6) is dark, tannic but well-padded with black cherry fruit, an old-fashioned Portuguese red made with care and style.

Vinho Verde: People who have holidayed in Portugal usually have fond memories of sitting in the sun with a glass of cool vinho verde. When they buy a bottle in the supermarket and open it on a November evening they are often surprised at how different it tastes. It just shows what sunshine and a holiday mood can do - make a very ordinary wine seem faintly magical. The best vinho verde are light, dry fresh and crisp - some are a touch fizzy but unimpressive. There's also red vinho verde - the 'verde' doesn't refer to the colour but to the countryside and the youth of the wine apparently - which has even less to recommend it.

SOUTH AFRICA

For various reasons, many of them political, a lot of South African wine has gone for distillation - not a destination that demands good winemaking or viticultural practices. The old Afrikaans refrain of 'maak die baak vol' or 'fill up the bin' was not just a harvest chorus but a pretty good indicator of the priorities. It was a terrible attitude, especially in a country which had once produced one of the world's most sought-after wines, the Black Muscat of Groot Constantia (which is undergoing a revival). Decades of self-imposed isolation meant that South Africa, as it clung to apartheid, denied itself access to markets where wine was subjected to very critical scrutiny. The giant KWV cooperative could only sell overseas but even they failed to bring home the message that the outside world wanted modern, cheap, attractive wines. But, having said that, in the days when the average Voortrekker liked nothing more than a sticky 'medium dry' white to go with the brai (the South African barbecue that appears to represent in its entirety the scope of Boer cuisine) Nederberg and KWV were the only producers of any size who were selling wines to people who were used to French, German and Italian styles. So, when sanctions disappeared, these two companies were ahead of the posse.

Now that South Africa has been welcomed into the civilised world, there is a great deal going on there. The mere handful of farsighted, foreign-trained winemakers of a few years back have been joined by hundreds of others whose horizons are set rather wider than the suburbs of Capetown.

KWV's Van Riebeeck (£4.99) range of varietals seems to represent the modern thrust of this giant co-operative. The Cabernet Sauvignon is good, crisp stuff, but the Pinotage gets my vote. It's spicy, surprisingly big and they manage to avoid that typical Elastoplast whiff that most Pinotage wines produce. The Sauvignon Blanc and Chenin Blanc are crisp, dry, fruity and very drinkable. The distinctly 'New World' style probably reflects the fact that the wines are grown in a highly fertile, irrigated region.

It can be argued that their contact with the outside world could have done more for their wines, but now, the KWV range have become more modern - particularly in the case of the white varietals, while maintaining a beefy kind of earthiness in the reds. Having said that, the style is evolving. The KWV range sells widely at between £4.99 and £5.99. Their crisp, fresh KWV Sauvignon Blanc and robust KWV Pinotage, which has the typical antiseptic twang on the nose, offering impressive value.

Two Oceans (£4.99) with a particularly ripe, full Cabernet Sauvignon and a light, easy-drinking Sauvignon Blanc are modern South African wines resolutely pointing the way forward, like Van Riebeeck, by giving us just what we want.

Nederberg is another great name in South Africa and their Cabernet Sauvignon 1991 (£4.99) is particularly successful. It even has a faintly Bordeaux character which is unusual in this neck of the woods. Nederberg Pinotage 1993 (£4.99) is surprisingly fruity, aromatic and true to the varietal character of this uniquely South African grape. Nederberg Sauvignon Blanc/Chardonnay 1994 (£4.99) doesn't really taste of either grape but it's a nice fresh concoction. Nederberg Chardonnay 1993 (£5.49) is very crisp, very lightly oaked and will appeal to anyone who likes the taste of Chablis but not the price.

Hamilton-Russell Pinot Noir 1992 (£10.09), a brick-coloured masterpiece expressing pure but complex Pinot character in a very attractive style is one of the most impressive South African reds I've yet encountered. One of the best Pinots outside Burgundy. The Chardonnay 1992 (£9.09) is a toasty, nutty number and a splendid buy.

Backsberg is an estate worth following and I have particularly liked the Chardonnay 1992 (£8.99) which has a stylish, buttery quality that suggests real quality. This is the kind of wine that prompts me to wonder if South Africa is remarkably well-suited to Chardonnay. There is also a juicy Pinotage and a soft, plummy Merlot which is not yet available here.

Try Meerlust Rubicon 1988 (£14.09) as an example of old-fashioned, upmarket South African winemaking. It's still rather tough, but there is great length and concentration there in a kind of claret style. Meerlust's Merlots are excellent wines with considerable structure and a distinctively varietal character, managing to achieve that kind of alcoholic-fruitcake style which often eludes New World winemakers.

Drosdty-Hof make delicious, fairly simple Chardonnay which are amongst South Africa's best buys provided you're not looking for big, buttery New World styles and their Sauvignon Blanc is an exercise in lightness and freshness. Alles Verloren Tinto Barocca is superb, made from one of the grapes that go into port, a huge, dark, sensationally concentrated wine with lots of tannic structure beneath generous fruit.

Neetlingshof make some superb but very expensive late harvest Rieslings which crop up occasionally on good restaurant lists. They even come in handy half bottles. But Neetlingshof Gewurztraminer (£5.99) is not only affordable but wonderfully aromatic. Dry yet luscious. When I first tasted it, I assumed it would cost twice the price.

Simonsig wines have been amongst the most attractive new arrivals of the last few months, particularly the Sauvignon Blanc 1992 (£5.99) and the big, soft, fruity Shiraz 1990 (£8.50)

Villiera Merlot 1990 (£9.09) is still a big, rather tannic wine which may well turn into something exceptional with time. Boschendal Sauvignon

Blanc 1992 (£6.99) is perhaps a bit too big and ripe for this varietal but lively acidity keeps it fresh and zesty.

Fleur du Cap (£6.99) make good modern red and white wines in a light, approachable style.

Quinnsworth's recently arrived Helderberg range is not very impressive, even at the price. The Chardonnay is a light, attractive commercial wine, while the rather wan Pinotage has a very antiseptic character on the nose which is true to the varietal. Douglas Green and Neil Ellis varietals are all pleasant but not much to write home about.

One of the world's best sparkling wines comes from the Bergkelder who also make Meerlust, Drosdty-Hof and Fleur du Cap. Pongracz Cape Sparkling (£12) may be hard to pronounce but it's made by the Champagne method from Pinot Noir and Chardonnay and allowed to mature on its lees. The result is a biscuity, yeasty, utterly delicious dry sparkling wine with real character. Certainly in the same league as Yalumba's Cuvee One and Mumm's Cuvée Napa. Seek it out.

SOUTH AMERICA

Although Argentina is South America's biggest wine producer, most of its wine production is more suited to the local taste for massive, strongly alcoholic red wines which Argentinians think go well with their famous beef, rather than the more sophisticated palates of export markets. Chile, on the other hand, has been capitalising like mad on the fact that vineyard workers come cheap and they don't have to spray against downy mildew because it is unknown in the country. As a result, they can afford to produce cheap, varietal wines and, thanks to a considerable French influence over the years, the wines are attuned to export markets. Actually, I think the Chileans could afford to do it even more cheaply if they put their minds to it. If it salves your conscience, the reason why you can buy southern French varietals at £4.99 which knock spots of many Chileans, it's because the French are heavily mechanised and don't have to pay vineyard workers at all - beyond a tiny handful on each estate. At least the Chilean labourers are employed, even if the pay is pretty pathetic.

A word about grape varieties. Malbec does particularly well in Argentina, one of the very few regions where it is bottled as a varietal. Sauvignon Blanc in Chile is more often than not Sauvignon Gris or Sauvignon Vert. They have lots of Sauvignon character when they are straight out of the fermentation tank but go into rapid decline. Always drink your Chilean Sauvignon Blanc as fresh as you can get it - otherwise you will end up with just a neutral, dry white wine.

Santa Rita and Concha y Toro were the first Chileans in Ireland. When Undurraga arrived it forced the price down to £4.99 and the Chilean revolution suddenly started to happen. It was so successful that the wines couldn't keep pace. Producers needed to plant vast hectarages and give them time to mature. Concha y Toro went off the boil, then Santa Rita.

Even Errazuriz went into decline. Now, Chile is getting its act together and most of the big names are back on form - some dramatically so.

Argentinian wines are a mixed bunch. At the time of the Falklands war a lot of dubious Argentinian grot got shifted over here by the UK agents. It was called Paral, and this was generally acknowledged to be short for Paralysis. However, Trapiche and Etchart are world-class, Flichman is starting to catch up. By comparison to Chile, Argentina is said to have massive potential in producing rather finer wines but investment and improvement is a slow business. A recent London tasting of excellent Argentinian wines from unknown producers revealed an unrealistic attitude to pricing which will keep them off the shelves until they realise how difficult it is to sell in a market as complex as ours. But it's a country worth watching.

Caliterra is part of the Errazuriz operation, specialists in high tech wine wizardry. The Cabernet/Sauvignon 1994 (QW £4.99) is quite attractive with some blackcurrant character, rather better in fact than the less defined impact of the Cabernet/Merlot 1994 (QW £4.99). The star, however, is the Cabernet Sauvignon Reserve 1992 (QW £6.69) with its rich, warm, berry flavours, subtle oak and decent length. Caliterra Sauvignon Blanc 1994 (QW £4.99) certainly appears to be the pick of the crop but the 1995 will be fresher when it arrives.

Canepa produce a bewilderingly large range which used to be exclusive to O'Brien's. Their Sauvignon Blanc (O'B £4.89) is not bad. Finissimo 1987 (£7.15) is not worth it. Canepa is now in broader distribution and the wines are said to be improving.

Carmen and Santa Rita are owned by the same company, but I reckon Carmen currently has a significant edge over its more famous sister. The Cabernet Sauvignon (SQ £4.99) is particularly elegant and attractive. There is a delicious Chardonnay (£5.99), a pleasant Sauvignon Blanc and a thunderingly good Merlot (£4.99) which manages to capture the luscious, soft, gulpable qualities of this grape in a particularly concentrated way.

Concha y Toro is one of the best-known Chilean names in Ireland and is still imported by Findlater's who pioneered Chilean wine here. For years I found the wines rather dull and old-fashioned but now, under a new winemaker, they are amongst the very best you can buy. The big, blockbuster Marques de Casa Concha (SQ £8.09) is a big Cabernet with lots of oak oomph while the flagship Don Melchior is one of the best reds from Chile today - full of blackcurrants and stylish oak, soft, ripe tannins and an impressively persistent finish. The cheaper wines are fresh, varietal, clean and satisfying.

Errazuriz wines, now made by a New Zealander, are getting back on form after a rather dull phase. The Sauvignon Blanc 1994 while lacking the ripeness of its Caliterra equivalent, and the Cabernet Sauvignon 1994 (£5.09) are textbook Chilean wines. Reserve Chardonnay and Cabernet Don Maximiano (£8.99) are certainly impressive but don't offer particularly outstanding value for money.

Etchart is a French-owned winery with the benefits of advice from their consultant winemaker, Robin Day or Australia's Orlando-Wyndham company. The Etchart Cafayate Torrontes (£4.99) is a glorious, aromatic, dry white wine which tastes like a Muscat but is in fact made from a native Argentinian grape. The reds are amongst Argentina's best, the Malbec (£5.99) simply delicious.

L.A. Cetto wines come all the way from Mexico. The raspberry-flavoured, dark Petite Syrah L.A. Cetto (SQ £6.99) with its jammy nose and lovely, easy, soft fruit is not a bad buy while the Sauvignon Blanc is a modest success. It will be sometime, I suspect, before we experience an invasion of other Mexican wines because these are, by general consent, held to be by far the best.

Los Vascos wines are singularly dull and best forgotten - despite the involvement of Chateau Lafite Rothschild. Perhaps the megabucks from France will pay dividends but we certainly have yet to see the results.

Montes are very serious producers, so how come the whites have become so ordinary? I don't know. But the remarkable Montes Alpha (£11.50) is one Chile's very finest Cabernets. The Merlot (£6.99) is pure fruit and absolutely delicious if lacking somewhat in tannic underpinning.

Navarro Correas make the kind of whopping, old-fashioned wines that Argentinians like to drink with their steaks. Cabernet Sauvignon Collecion Privada 1988 (McC £12.99) is huge, a bit coarse but quite a mouthful all the same. The price is crazy. The equivalent Pinot Noir is a weird wine.

Santa Carolina, like Concha y Toro, is one of Chiles most important names and their winemaker is a revolutionary in terms of quality and innovation - so much so that Senor Recabarren has become the country's first flying winemaker. The wines are mainly restaurant based in Ireland. Both the Cabernet Sauvignon Reserve and the Sauvignon Blanc Reserve are outstanding. However, the wine for me, is the Merlot Reserve 1990 (McC £7.99) - rich, ripe and elegant with a touch of Pomerol class about it.

Santa Ines make virtually all of their wines from grapes grown on their own estates and this gives them considerable control over quality. Definitely one of Chile's most serious producers with excellent Cabernets and a surprisingly ripe Sauvignon Blanc.

Santa Rita's Sauvignon Blanc 120 (£5.09) is one of the best in its class but the equivalent Merlot is rather lean and tannic. Watch out for the Cabernet Sauvignon Medalla Real 1993 (£8.09) - Michael Broadbent describes it as having 'an almost Petrus-like opulence.' Another cracker is the Chardonnay Casanova 1990 (MO £9.09) while the Cabernet Sauvignon Santa Rita Casa Real 1989 (SQ £14.99) is without doubt the finest wine that Chile currently produces.

Torres have taken quite a long time to get their Chilean operation right. For years the wines were simply woeful. But now their Santa Digna Sauvignon Blanc 1994 (£5.99) is right up with the best of them and the equivalent Cabernet manages to be both fresh and ripe at the same time. But the most exciting new wine to come out of Torres, let alone Chile, in the past two years or so, has been the sensational Cabernet Sauvignon Manso de Velsaco 1989 (£8.99). It has fabulously concentrated cassis fruit, slightly austere French oak and an overwhelming sense of quality and style. Santa Rita's Casa Real should watch its back!

Trapiche is Argentina's biggest producer of quality wines and has been a leader in reforming viticultural and winemaking practices. A few years ago I tasted disappointingly dilute Chardonnay which their export director was enthusing about. But now their Oak Cask Reserve Chardonnay (DS£5.99) is probably the single best value white wine coming out of South America - with its toasty oaky, pleasant fruit, lovely balance and decent concentration. Trapiche Malbec Reserve 1989 (SQ £4.99) offers a great opportunity to taste this particular varietal on its own with just a hint of new oak to fill out the picture. It underlines very effectively how Argentina has taken this Bordeaux grape variety and learned to love it.

Undurraga makes a delicious, almost aggressively aromatic Sauvignon Blanc 1994 (SQ £4.99, w £5.09) which is marred, for me, by rather aggressive acidity on the finish. The Cabernet Sauvignon 1991 is pleasant, while the Cabernet Sauvignon Reserve 1990 (£6.99) is chunky but rather too baked for my liking.

Valdezaro wines (£3.99) are particularly lean and dull.

S P A I N

Spain has more land under vine than any other country in the world, but it is only the third largest producer. Much of Spain is so hot and arid that the vines produce remarkably low yields. With enormous domestic demand and a huge tourist trade, many Spanish producers have been able to get away with making creaking old oxidised rubbish and find a ready market for it. But times are changing. Joining the EU in 1986 has meant that Spain has had to get its act together and the country now has a pretty sophisticated system of wine laws.

There is also a new willingness to use modern, clean, temperature-controlled winemaking techniques and a resultant leap in general standards. Now, everybody is looking to the pioneers of quality. It would seem that the recession has really concentrated minds.

The places that seem to be really hot - in wine terms as well as climate - are Ribero del Duero at the top end of the market, and Navarra at the more accessible end. But there are great things happening, too, in Rueda and Alella and even good old La Mancha is stirring into life and leaving the dull, flat, crude, oxidised image behind.

Of course Spain's most under-rated wine is sherry. Not the sweet 'n sticky, faintly brown big label stuff so beloved of the most unlikely Christmas tipplers but the serious wines like bone dry finos, manzanillas and amontillados and the luscious dessert olorosos and palo cortados.

Alella: These vineyards, near Barcelona, produce fruity white wines, the best undoubtedly coming from the Marques de Alella whose Classico (MO£6.99) is a refreshing, quite big and fleshy blend of Chenin Blanc and Pansa Blanca. The Allier (MO £13.99) is a magnificent, ultra-ripe pure Chardonnay aged in French oak and well worth seeking out if

114

you're looking for a Burgundy beater.

Carinena: Nothing to get over-excited about here but Don Mendo and Monte Ducay deliver typical if unsubtle oaky reds which are cheaper than similar Rioja.

Cava: This is Spanish sparkling wine, invented by a Senor Raventos and made by a somewhat modified version of the Champagne method. Cava producers need to get their act together or the New World will have them for breakfast. Plantings of Chardonnay are on the increase, but virtually all Cava is still made from Macabeo, Xarel-lo and Parellada which simply don't add up to serious sparkling wine. And why do they always have a faint smell of burnt rubber? Codorniu (£7.99), Rondel (SQ £7.99) and Parxet are fine but not exactly exciting. Freixnet Cordon Negro has managed to achieve a surprising elegance, while Segura Viudas is very over-rated.

Costers del Segre: There are treasures here, especially from the amazingly high-tech winery of Raimat which is owned by the Raventos family of Codorniu fame. It's a desert, in effect, that has been made to bloom. Raimat Abadia 1991 (£8.49) is a Cabernet, Tempranillo and Garnacha blend, very ripe and juicy and with plenty of vanilla-like American oak. Raimat Cabernet Sauvignon (£8.50) is intensely blackcurranty with a firm tannin backbone and lots of structure. Raimat Chardonnay 1992 (£7.79) is ripe, typical and unwooded but nice and crisp.

Jumilla: Try the pungent, dark, red Taja 1992 (SN £6.80), produced by Frank Mahler-Besse, co-owner of the great Margaux property, Chateau Palmer.

La Mancha: Mainly a source of plonk for the bars of Madrid. La Taberna (S £3.99) is one of the better examples. Allozo Tempranillo Crianza 1991 (QW £4.99) is rather flabby, but not bad at the price.

Navarra: This is a vast area close to Rioja where many exciting things are happening including the gradual ousting of the workhorse red grape Garnacha by Cabernet Sauvignon. Don Carlos Navarra Oak-Aged Red 1992 (£5.49) is a Tempranillo/Cabernet blend with a whiff of vanilla. The equivalent white is a blend of Chardonnay and the native Viura, barrel fermented. Both wines have a surprising degree of style for the price. The most famous name in the region is Ochoa whose rich, spicy, oaky, slightly strawberryish Tempranillo Crianza 1992 (SQ £5.69) offers what can only be described as outstanding value. Ochoa Reserva 1986 (£8.25) and Gran Reserva 1985 (£9.69) are as good as many a similarly priced Rioja - but with slightly firmer tannins in the background.

Penedes: As every wine buff knows, Torres is not only the greatest commercial name in Penedes. The same can be said also of Spain in general. Torres is obsessively quality conscious, high-tech, innovative and adventurous. But what has been happening to the wines? Has Torres lost its way? As far as I can make out, Torres is going through a bad patch. The wines are certainly not bad but they lack the excitement that once characterised the name. A touch too much caution? An exception has to be Vina Magdala 1990 (SQ £7.25) - Pinot Noir with a small dash of Tempranillo for colour. It has a faintly musky nose, with classic 'farmyard' smells (this is the polite way of putting it), spicy oak, cedarwood and that elusive cherryish taste of Pinot coming through. It's a most unusual wine - probably not to everyone's taste - but I think it's delicious and amazingly well-priced. I like the grapey charm of Viña Esmeralda 099). Gran Viña Sol Chardonnay 1993 (£6.99) has a nice touch of oak and decent fruit - not a bad buy at the price. But the upmarket Fransola (£11.00) which incorporates over-ripe Sauvignon Blanc is, to me, a bit of a mess. Gran Coronas Reserva 1988 (£7.99) is surprisingly thin and short - a vintage problem? Frankly, Torres' Manso de Velasco from Chile puts the current Spanish output in the shade.

Jean Leon produces a Californian-inspired Cabernet and Chardonnay -

Penedes, of course, can look remarkably like California. Leon's wines are always dear but equally stylish. They seem to have vanished from the Irish market for the time being.

Masia Bach, like Raimat, is owned by the huge Codorniu Cava company. They make a highly attractive, lightish, gulpable Cabernet Sauvignon 1989 (£6.29) which has everything you want: lots of ripe blackcurrant fruit, crisp, fresh acidity and just enough oak.

Priorato: Connoisseur's wine with buckets of alcohol. The Don Carlos Priorato Gran Reserva 1987 (SQ/RS £10.99) is one of the rarest wines in the world, made exclusively from ancient garnacha vines in the high Penedes at the legendary winery of Scala Dei. It's still rather tough and hotly alcoholic but, like another beverage, worth waiting for. How long? Two to three years should see it reaching an earthy perfection. Open it a few hours before drinking and let it reach room temperature - even a day ahead. There is quite an amount of tartrate deposit in this wine, so stand it upright for a few hours and either pour very carefully or take the bull by the horns and decant it.

Rias Baixas: Santiago Ruiz's Rias Baixas is probably the best wine from this white-producing region in Galicia. With its distinctive doodled label, stg£10 price tag and elegant intensity, Santiago Ring is not only King Juan Carlos' favourite tipple (if you want to know) but an immensely attractive alternative to the tidal wave of Chardonnay and Sauvignon Blanc. So far available only in Northern Ireland.

Ribiera del Duero: This is home to Spain's most distinguished winery, Vega Sicilia, whose wines are so rare and expensive as to be of similarly academic interest as the Bordeaux first growths. They are made from the Bordeaux classic varietals, Cabernet Sauvignon, Cabernet Franc and Merlot, and are aged in new American oak casks. The Valbueno (£35) strikes me as being rather over-priced while the Unico 1979 (£80) is one of the greatest wines I've ever tasted. The combination of concentration, length and sheer style is breathtaking.

The highly fashionable Pesquera Crianza 1989 (SN£9.99) is now available from Searson's. This is the wine which, alas, Robert Parker, the American guru, described as being the 'Spanish Petrus.' Hence the fabulous prices.

Every bit as good as Pesquera Crianza, I reckon, is the Pago de Carraovejas 1992 (SN £9.60) - dark, intense, complex, oaky, velvety, long. The rich, plummy, faintly Merlot-ish Senorio de Nava Crianza 1989 (SQ £6.99) actually contains no Merlot at all but, like all wines from this region, depends on Tinto Fino (known elsewhere as Tempranillo) for its silkiness. The ultra-modern Durius red (£4.99) is made by the Marques de Grinon and delivers good soft, ripe fruit with a reasonable backbone at a very decent price. Solana 1993 Ribeiro Blanco Torrontes e Treixadura 1994 (SQ £5.99) is fresh, dry and grapeily Muscat-like.

Rioja: The first time I realised that rioja could be sublime was when I tasted the Marques de Arienzo Gran Reserva 1976 when visiting the Domecq sherry bodega in 1986. An amazing wine, quite unforgettable. I keep trying to recapture the experience but, so far, without success.

Part of the problem is that demand for Rioja during the 1980s seriously outstripped supply and a lot of dull, stretched, poorly-made wine has hit the market. Hence, it's important to be selective.

The most dependable names, I have found in the last year or so, to be Marques de Murrieta, Faustino, Campo Viejo, Marques de Grinon, Montecillo, Marques de Caceres, Olarra and, more recently, the born-again, bolder Marques de Riscal.

The best news from Rioja in a long time has been the arrival of the Marques de Grinon Crianza 1989 (£5.99). Made by the legendary Carlos

Falco, this is a 100% Tempranillo wine with lovely colour, a bewitching combination of berry fruit and lightly toasty oak on the nose, velvet fruit and good length. The only problem is, I gather, that it's in very short supply. I've also enjoyed Navajas Reserva 1987 (SN£7.95) but supplies have already dried up. A name to watch, however.

La Rioja Alta is one of the most serious producers with stunningly classic, concentrated wines like the currently available 1983 Gran Reserva 904 (£18.99) This is amongst the best Riojas I've ever tasted - with a degree of complexity I would normally associate with fine claret. La Rioja Alta's Viña Alberdi Crianza 1989 (£8.49) may appear dear for a humble crianza but this stuff is better than most house's reservas. Best known of the range, I suspect, is the glorious Viña Ardanza Reserva 1987 (£14.29) with its masses of fruit supporting a whooping amount of integrated, spicy American oak. A classic.

Campo Viejo is one of Rioja's biggest producers and has been known to deliver excellent value for money. Just at present, I have a feeling the wines are not quite as good as they have been. Worth watching, though.

Don Carlos Rioja Reserva 1987 (£7.99) is, in fact, the wine of Baron de Ley - has started to open up nicely.

Contino Rioja Reserva 1987, the flagship of the CUNE company, (SQ £12.99) is not worth the price but remains an elegant wine for all that. However, I've had rather too many corky bottles. The CUNE Imperial Reserva 1987 (£12.99) is excellent, coming within shouting distance of the great Viña Ardanza. Even the basic crianzas are sound.

One of the best value gran reservas has to be the Montecillo Viña Monty Gran Reserva 1985/86 (£8.69), while one of the most disappointing labels, I have found, is Monte Real.

Is Faustino resting a little on its laurels? I find it hard to say but there's no doubt that the wines are very consistent. The bottle looks so naff and the Gran Reserva 1987 (£10.85) is so popular with a certain kind of consumer that I usually avoid this marque. But whenever I get round to tasting it I'm usually impressed with the stuff. Faustino VII (£5.39) is a good, simple, cheap stuff while their Roblejano table wine (SQ£4.49) has reasonable fruit and a vanilla character imparted by oak chips (or 'tea bags' as they call them in the business) and there's no shame in it at this price.

Nobody seems to rate Bodegas Bordon in the first flight of Rioja houses and I have to admit that some of their younger wines lack pzazz. However, they release small quantities of older wines which are often both fascinating and delicious. Bordon Gran Reserva 1964 (£17) is very elegant if tiring a little, while the 1973 (£15) is delicious right now. Outstanding value for money.

Berberana is a sound value for money house with a particularly attractive bargain in its Tempranillo Rioja 1993 (QW £4.99).

Rueda: Source of Spain's most modern and high tech white wines of which two examples demand attention. Yet to arrive in the South is the Bordeaux-owned Hermanos Lurton Sauvignon Blanc 1993 (JN stg£4.99) which is packed with fresh, cool, zingy, zesty fruit and is almost New Zealand in its potent varietal character. From the same stable as the eponymous Rioja comes the less exciting and perhaps a little over-priced Marques de Riscal Sauvignon 1994 Rueda (F £7.99) which is nonetheless quite a wine. The white Durius (£4.99) from the Marques de Grinon is a textbook modern, fresh, light white wine.

Sherry: Sherry has developed a bad name, largely because of the awful dross that goes into the average sweet commercial blend. The most exciting sherries are dry. Try one of the superb finos: Tio Pepe, San Patricio, La Ina all of which are widely available. Then graduate to the stunning almacenista sherries from Lustau which are stocked by Mitchell's. Williams and Humbert's Dos Cortados (£12.99 MO/T) is that rarest of sherries, a palo cortado: nutty, complex, bone dry, superb. Try Searson's for small quantities of stunning, old dessert sherries.

Sonmontano One of the most exciting emerging wine regions represented here by the Vinas del Rey range from the San Marco estate. The Chenin Blanc 1994(£5.79) is crisp, flowery and almost bone dry. The Gewurztraminer 1993 (£5.79) is a classic lychees-and-spice job with oodles of fruit, apparently a little sweet at first but when you analyse it on your palate it comes across quite dry. The barrel-fermented Chardonnay 1993 (£7.99) is very vanilla-dominated with a certain nutty European restraint allied to distinctly New World butterscotch undertones. Tempranillo/Cabernet Sauvignon 1991(£5.79) is lovely - the Tempranillo's ripe, strawberry fruit taking the tannic edge off the more austere but distinctly blackcurrant Cabernet - with a curiously creamy/vanilla dimension. A Merlot/Cabernet Sauvignon Reserva 1991 (£8.99) blend has even more fruit and even more oak, making it a big, gutsy but still soft and rounded wine.

Tarragona: Everything I've tasted from this Catalonian region has been pretty gruesome. We live in hope of improvements. Much of Tarragona's production is exported as fortified altar wine while its ordinary whites often end up in Cava.

Toro: This is a newly emerging region in the North West, characterised by big, high alcohol red wines. Of the few which are available in Ireland, many are clumsy, hot and jammy. The safest bet is to stick to the wines of Bodegas Farina whose Collegiata Tinto 1991 (£5.99) is rich, ripe and surprisingly gentle despite its massive 14.5% alcohol. Gran Collegiata Reserva 1989 (£6.99) is in similar vein but with a much more apparent oaky character. Less fine but still a decent mouthful are the wines from one of the major co-operatives: Valdeoliva (£4.59), dark, chewy and hot,

Cermeno (£4.99) which is lightly oaked, and the chunky, oaky Canusverus (£6.99).

Valdepeñas: The home of soft, often dull, oaky red wines. However, the top producers certainly deliver value for money. Vina Albali (SQ £3.99) is the only oaky wine I know at the price. Senorio de los Llanos and Don Carlos are synonymous in this region and the Gran Reserva (£7.99) is a nice, soft, easy wine which perhaps needs a bit more fruit to balance the heavy oak influence.

Valencia: This is a source of undistinguished reds and whites, by and large, of which Castillo de Liria (QW £3.99) is probably the best - and quite decent at the price. Moscatel de Valencia Marks & Spencer (MS £4.99) is a beautifully aromatic, light dessert wine at a remarkably good price.

Yecla: There's not much of it around but beware the crude wines of the curiously-named La Purisma co-operative which I've always found as dull as ditchwater. Instead, try the pleasantly smooth, rounded but otherwise not exactly electrifying Pozuelo Crianza 1990 (MW £5.99).

index

Tom Doorley is *uncorked* every week in

Tribune The Sunday

If your would like to read more of Tom Doorley, you can
– every week in the Tribune Magazine,
which comes free with The Sunday Tribune.
Tom writes two columns – on wine and food – for the Magazine
which is also home to Joe O'Connor (humour),
Helen Dillon (gardening), Deirdre McQuillan (fashion),
Diarmuid Doyle (TV), Ciaran Carty (film),
Aodhgan Feeley (an antedote to Dublin 4)
plus books, arts and all the lifestyle and human interest features
you can expect from Ireland's quality Sunday newspaper.